IS THE
END
NEAR?

WHAT

JESUS

TOLD US

ABOUT THE

LAST DAYS

IS THE END NEAR?

MICHAEL YOUSSEF

Visit the author's website at ltw.org, dryoussefbooks.com.

Cataloging-in-Publication Data is on file with the Library of Congress.
International Standard Book Number: 978-1-63641-091-3
E-book ISBN: 978-1-63641-092-0

22 23 24 25 26 — 987654321
Printed in the United States of America

To all my ministry partners around the world, without whom this ministry would not be possible

CONTENTS

FOREWORD

O F ALL DR. Michael Youssef's many books, I feel singularly honored to be asked to write the foreword to this one. It is right up my street—and there is no subject that grips me more, challenges me more, and gives me more hope.

The answer to the question "Is the end near?" is yes. If you have any doubts about this, get ready to receive information that will not only convince you but sober you to your fingertips. At the same time, this book will equip you not to be afraid. There is so much to look forward to, and you won't have to wait long! There is a lot coming down the road that is not pleasant. This includes persecution as our nation has not seen. But such persecution elevates us to a higher level—approaching what the great saints of old experienced. Why should you and I be exempt? Our being shoved out of our comfort zones is long overdue, and the result will be joy and victory beyond anything we could have dreamed.

Beginning with the helpful analogy of a woman in labor pains just before the arrival of her baby, Dr. Youssef demonstrates that today we are in that very moment. This helps you and me understand what is going on at the present time. We are right in the middle of that painful time when we await God's stepping in—which He does in the nick of time. For example, Dr. Youssef shows six labor pains from Matthew 24. These are unfolded and applied so clearly and helpfully. This kind of clarity continues throughout the book. This book provides the most practical and relevant application of Matthew 24 I have ever read.

There is more: this book is filled with vital information—not just Dr. Youssef's theological convictions but scientific facts, relevant knowledge. With his wide and careful research, Dr. Youssef has gifted us with helpful information that shows he is in touch with what is going on in the world. I have learned things that I hardly expected from this kind of book.

A further subsidiary fallout of this book could be that Christians will be stirred to pray like never before—so much so that it could lead to great revival just before the end.

—R. T. Kendall

Chapter 1

IS THIS THE END?

INCREASINGLY PEOPLE BOTH within and outside the church are asking the same question: Is this the end of the world? Christians phrase it differently, of course: Are we in the end-time? But both Christians and non-Christians are watching current events and coming to the same conclusion: history appears to be drawing to a culmination.

In July 2021 *The Nation* published a story titled "The End of the World Is Closer Than It Seems." In that piece author Tom Engelhardt wrote that he worries the world will end in a nuclear holocaust. Even as a pandemic killed millions in 2020, nine nations, he points out, were growing their nuclear arsenals. More than half of the expenditures for new nuclear weaponry—$37.4 billion—were laid out by the United States, including $13.3 billion for the development of intercontinental ballistic missiles. In total the nine nuclear-armed nations spent about $137,000 per minute to update a global nuclear arsenal that, Engelhardt writes, "could end history as we know it."[1]

That same month, in the *Telegraph* of Great Britain, columnist Janet Daley wrote, "Is this the end of the world? Every time I turn on the television news I am confronted by an apocalyptic panorama of fire, flood and never-ending plague." Though Daley didn't believe the world would end in fire, flood, or plague, she worried that a frightened humanity might be stampeded into accepting "an authoritarianism that presents itself as benign" but inevitably proves to be tyrannical.[2] If you have read the Bible prophecies of the Antichrist, you know what this "authoritarianism" would look like.

Also in 2021 the *Chicago Maroon*, the independent student newspaper of The University of Chicago, published a story titled "Is This the End of the World?," in which authors Milutin Gjaja and Laura Gersony trace the origin of the Doomsday Clock—a warning symbol of global catastrophe. The clock was created in 1947 by the scientists who helped develop the first atomic weapons in World War II. Their publication, the *Bulletin of the Atomic Scientists*, has shown the Doomsday Clock on the cover of every issue. The clock, housed at the University of Chicago's Harris School of

Public Policy, illustrates the scientists' assessment of the extinction threat to humanity.

On the Doomsday Clock midnight symbolizes ultimate doom, the end of humanity. The first cover of the *Bulletin of the Atomic Scientists*, in 1947, showed the clock's hands at seven minutes to midnight. Over the years, those hands have sometimes moved closer to midnight and sometimes farther away, based on the assessment of experts. The clock moved to two minutes before midnight in 1953 after the development of the hydrogen bomb and swung to seventeen minutes before midnight at the end of the Cold War, in 1991.

Gjaja and Gersony listed numerous threats to humanity: a global pandemic, wildfires, hurricanes, climate change, and even swarms of locusts "of biblical proportions" that decimated crops in East Africa. These disasters seemed to explode at the beginning of the 2020s. As I write these words, the Doomsday Clock displays a sobering one hundred seconds to humanity's midnight. In the estimation of these experts, the threat to humanity has never been greater than it is right now.[3]

In the coming pages we're going to look at some of the horrors and catastrophes that threaten the human race—and that Jesus told us would come upon the world before His return. If you are an unbeliever and you are looking realistically at the state of the world right now, I honestly don't know how you can sleep at night. But if you are a genuine follower of Christ, you can face the future without fear. You don't need to cower under your bed, because God is in control of this world—and He is in control of your life.

The book you hold in your hands is not intended to frighten you but to encourage you, give you hope, and magnify your joy. It is almighty God, not the atomic scientists, who holds the future in His hands. His timetable never moves forward or backward with changing events. In His Word, God has given us a reliable and reassuring guide to the future. Jesus has told us what to expect in the days before His return, and He has told us not to be anxious or afraid.

Wars and Rumors of Wars

What events did Jesus foretell? As we are about to see, He prophesied that false messiahs would come, deceiving many. Wars and rumors of wars would spread around the globe. Nations, political rulers, and ethnic groups would rise up against one another. Famines would decimate populations, and earthquakes would shake the earth. Jesus foretold all these horrors—and they are coming to pass as I write these words.

In the decades since the end of the Cold War, people have become complacent, assuming that it was unthinkable that one nation would invade another nation, as Nazi Germany invaded Poland, France, and other nations in World War II. Then, on February 24, 2022, after amassing a force of 190,000 troops along the Ukrainian border, Russia brazenly attacked Ukraine, bent on slaughtering civilians and swallowing up the entire country.[4] This act of unprovoked aggression, ordered by Russian dictator Vladimir Putin, triggered the largest European refugee crisis since World War II, displacing nearly seven million people, about one-sixth of the Ukrainian population.[5]

Russian atrocities against the Ukrainian people included the indiscriminate slaughter of civilians, acts of rape and pillaging by Russian soldiers, and the deliberate targeting of a bomb shelter in Mariupol that was clearly marked "Children." Three hundred Ukrainian civilians, including many children, died in the attack.[6]

A viral video from Ukraine shows a little girl with a message scrawled on her bare back. As bombs and artillery shells rained down upon this child's neighborhood, her tearful mother took a marker and wrote the child's name and birth date, along with the phone numbers of her parents, on her back. Many Ukrainian mothers and fathers have had to prepare for the unthinkable—the very real possibility that they and their children might be separated or killed as war engulfs their country.[7]

INFLATION, SCARCITY, AND FAMINE

Even before the war in Ukraine, the world economy was staggering from the effects of more than two years of the COVID-19 pandemic. The pandemic had scrambled the supply chain, bankrupted businesses, and fueled uncontrolled inflation. In 2020 David M. Beasley, executive director of the UN's World Food

Programme, predicted that the pandemic would cause "famines of biblical proportions" in more than thirty developing countries. "This is truly more than just a pandemic," Beasley said. "It is creating a hunger pandemic. This is a humanitarian and food catastrophe."[8]

What Beasley didn't know and could not have foreseen was that the food catastrophe of 2020 would be made many times worse by the Ukraine war in 2022. Russia's invasion of Ukraine prompted the United States and Europe to boycott Russian oil, gas, grain, seafood, and other exports.[9] War-torn Ukraine, once the world's largest wheat exporter, stopped shipping its harvest, resulting in abrupt food shortages around the world.[10]

The global boycott of exports from Russia and its ally Belarus had a devastating impact on global food production. Before the war, Russia and Belarus supplied much of the world's agricultural fertilizer needs, including more than 40 percent of the world's agricultural potash, 22 percent of the world's agricultural ammonia, 14 percent of the world's urea, and 14 percent of the world's monoammonium phosphate. These fertilizers are essential to growing corn, soy, rice, and wheat. From Canada to Brazil, from Africa to China, growers faced shortages of essential soil nutrients—and populations faced famine. In just one month following the Russian invasion of Ukraine, global wheat prices climbed 21 percent, barley prices 33 percent, and fertilizer prices 40 percent. Tony Will, CEO of American fertilizer producer CF Industries, told Reuters, "My concern at the moment is actually one of a food crisis on a global basis."[11]

The UN's Beasley said Russia's invasion of Ukraine "has only compounded a catastrophe on top of a catastrophe. There is no precedent even close to this since World War II."[12] And US president Joe Biden warned, "It's going to be real. The price of the sanctions is not just imposed upon Russia. It's imposed upon an awful lot of countries as well, including European countries and our country as well."[13]

Jesus told us that before His return we would witness wars and famines. These crises are coming upon the world right now. They are already devastating the world economy and the lives of countless people around the world.

A Bag With Holes in It

The Lord has warned that out-of-control inflation is a sign of divine judgment against disobedience. The prophet Haggai said, "Now this is what the LORD Almighty says: 'Give careful thought to your ways. You have planted much, but harvested little. You eat, but never have enough. You drink, but never have your fill. You put on clothes, but are not warm. You earn wages, only to put them in a purse with holes in it'" (Hag. 1:5–6).

When you go to the supermarket or gas station, isn't that exactly what it feels like—that you've been keeping your wages in a bag with holes in it? That's the impact of inflation on your earnings, investments, and net worth.

For decades a healthy, roaring global economy has been creating jobs, producing wealth, and reducing poverty. People around the world have enjoyed stable prices. That began to change with the global pandemic that started in China and spread around the world. In response governments panicked and shut down businesses and commerce. Around the world families began driving less, tightening grocery budgets, and economizing wherever possible.

To compensate for lost jobs and lost wages, the US government issued a series of direct payments to its citizens. These so-called "stimulus checks" increased the money supply (and the national debt) with borrowed money, producing what some economists call "an overheated economy," fueling still more inflation.[14]

In March 2022 four economists at the Federal Reserve of San Francisco issued a report showing that these "stimulus checks" had worsened an already surging inflation rate. In February 2022 the annualized inflation rate in the United States had reached 7.9 percent, a forty-year high—and considerably higher than in France (3.6 percent), Germany (5.1 percent), and the United Kingdom (5.5 percent), countries that did *not* issue checks to their citizens.

Larry Summers, who served as a White House economic adviser in the Obama administration, warned

Congress and the White House in early 2021. He predicted these direct payments would "set off inflationary pressures of a kind we have not seen in a generation"—but politicians didn't listen.

Many of those payments went to people earning up to $160,000 in joint income. The Federal Reserve economists stated that these payments resulted in too much money chasing too few goods and services—and the result was soaring inflation. The economists concluded, "U.S. income transfers may have contributed to an increase in inflation of about 3 percentage points by the fourth quarter of 2021."[15]

A Day's Worth of Subsistence

Along with soaring inflation and increasing scarcity comes the specter of global famine. Many Bible scholars see a correlation between the Lord's prophecy of a famine in the last days and the apostle John's prophecy of the third seal of judgment in Revelation 6:

> When the Lamb opened the third seal, I heard the third living creature say, "Come!" I looked, and there before me was a black horse! Its rider was holding a pair of scales in his hand. Then I heard what sounded like a voice among the four living creatures, saying, "Two pounds of wheat for a day's wages, and six pounds of barley for a day's wages, and do not damage the oil and the wine!"
>
> —Revelation 6:5–6

This is a prophecy of widespread inflation, poverty, and hunger. In ancient times two pounds of wheat was considered enough to keep one person alive for one day. In this prophecy a person would have to work for a full day to earn enough money to buy one day's worth of food. In other words, a person would have to work all day just to keep body and soul together.

Most American workers are accustomed to making enough money to buy not only food but restaurant meals, expensive café coffee, a good car, and a nice home, as well as pay for plenty of entertainment. The day may arrive soon when a full day's work will only buy a day's worth of subsistence—perhaps a loaf of bread and no more.

And notice that statement "and do not damage the oil and the wine!" Olive oil, in Bible times, was not only a food but a fuel, used to light lamps. It may be that this statement in Revelation is a hint that in the last days oil for fuel may become a scarcity, a luxury that few can afford. We are already seeing the price of gasoline and other oil-based products soaring to heights we have never witnessed before, primarily as a result of a global boycott of Russian petroleum. The global boycott of Russian exports is morally right—but it will likely lead to rising energy costs, increasing scarcity, and more inflation.

"It's Not Going to End"

How long will Russia's war against Ukraine last? In early February 2022, General Mark Milley, chairman of the Joint Chiefs of Staff, briefed US lawmakers on the massing of Russian troops on the Ukrainian border. He predicted that if Russia launched a full-scale invasion of Ukraine, the capital city, Kyiv, could fall within seventy-two hours.[16] Within a couple of weeks of the Russian invasion beginning, on February 24, Ukrainian forces astonished the world—and shocked the Russians—by forcing the invaders to retreat and regroup. By March 11 Ukraine had destroyed 353 Russian tanks.[17]

Two months later General Milley reversed his prediction. In early April 2022 he told the US House Armed Services Committee, "I do think this is a very protracted conflict, and I think it's measured in years. I don't know about decade, but at least years for sure."[18]

Ian Bremmer is a political scientist and founder of the Eurasia Group. He specializes in assessing global political risk. In April 2022 he was a guest on a popular podcast, where he talked about the future of Russia's war against Ukraine. "There is going to be a new Iron Curtain," he said, adding, "When people ask me, 'How is this going to end?' my view is, 'What do you mean, end? It's not going to end. We're going to have a much more unstable global order.'"

The host asked Bremmer if there is anything Western nations can do to force Russia to withdraw from Ukraine.

Bremmer replied, "We are going to hurt the Russian economy structurally. Russia will be in a depression. Their GDP will contract by 10 to 15 percent at a minimum. That's a big deal. But will [Russian President Vladimir] Putin be forced to behave differently in Ukraine? Will he be forced to capitulate because of the sanctions? I think the answer to that is clearly no....This is why I'm so pessimistic about where this crisis is going."[19]

As the war in Ukraine continues, so will global instability. Experts see no end in sight—no end to the war, no end to our troubled economy, no end to inflation. Russia's attack on Ukraine has caused a profound restructuring of the political and trade relationships between the East and the West. The tense standoff has become a new Iron Curtain that may well exist throughout our lifetime—or until the Lord's return.

It's unlikely that we will ever see the world go back to the relatively peaceful and cooperative era that followed the Cold War. A new and more dangerous Cold War has begun. Russia—a nakedly aggressive and hostile nation—is one of the five permanent members of the United Nations Security Council, with absolute veto power over any resolutions that body may make. Another permanent member of the Security Council is China, which openly and frequently voices its plans to subjugate the free nation of Taiwan. Together, Russia and China present the greatest threat to global peace and stability and have turned the United Nations into a powerless, meaningless debate club.

Some Bible interpreters believe that both Russia and China figure prominently in Bible prophecy. The prophet Ezekiel foretold that in the last days there will be a great war and the army of a powerful nation from the north will descend upon Israel. The prince of that nation is called Gog, and the nation itself is called Magog—and Magog is widely believed to represent Russia. Ezekiel writes:

> The word of the LORD came to me: "Son of man, set your face against Gog, of the land of Magog, the chief prince of Meshek and Tubal; prophesy against him and say: 'This is what the Sovereign LORD says: I am against you, Gog, chief prince of Meshek and Tubal. I will turn you around, put hooks in your jaws and bring you out with your whole army—your horses, your horsemen fully armed, and a great horde with large and small shields, all of them brandishing their swords.'...
>
> "Therefore, son of man, prophesy and say to Gog: 'This is what the Sovereign LORD says: In that day, when my people Israel are living in safety, will you not take notice of it? You will come from your place in the far north, you and many nations with you, all of them riding on horses, a great horde, a mighty army. You will advance against my people Israel like a cloud that covers the land.'"
>
> —EZEKIEL 38:1–4, 14–16

In the place where God, speaking through the prophet Ezekiel, says that he opposes the "chief prince of Meshek and Tubal," some translators, including those of the New American Standard Bible, render that phrase "the prince of Rosh, Meshech and Tubal." Rosh was one of the sons of Benjamin (Gen. 46:21), and some Bible scholars suggest that Rosh may have settled far to the north of Israel. The name Rosh may have become Rus', the ancient Norse-Slavic word from which we derive the modern word Russia (though this is highly conjectural).

This passage in Ezekiel probably foretells a future attack by Russia against Israel—an attack that ultimately leads to Russia's judgment and destruction by God. It is interesting to note that Moscow is about 1,660 miles due north of Jerusalem—and there is nothing to the north of Russia but the polar ice cap. So when God says to Magog, "You will come from your place in the far north," it is hard to imagine who else He might be speaking of except Russia.

I would hasten to add that God has not given us many details of the future events to take place in what we call the end-time. There is much in the prophecy of Ezekiel 38 and 39 that is hard to understand, just as there is in the Lord's discourse in Matthew 24 and 25. Above all, we must be careful not to set a timetable for future events. The Lord may return at any moment—or He may not return for thousands of years.

God didn't give biblical prophecy to us so we could

know exactly what is to happen and when it will take place. God gave biblical prophecy to instruct us and encourage us to live holy lives. He wants us to live obediently, watching and ready for His return whenever the heavens open and Jesus appears. We don't know the day or the hour—but we know what God has called us to do.

"Gradually and Then Suddenly"

Many catastrophes unleashed upon the human race are caused by human beings. Some argue the COVID-19 pandemic was likely spawned by gain-of-function experimentation—research that seeks to modify a biological pathway in a cell line or organism[20]—on bat viruses at the Wuhan Institute of Virology in Wuhan, China. Russia's unprovoked war against Ukraine was a scheme hatched in the murderous thoughts of one powerful Russian ruler.

Another human-caused catastrophe has been approaching for years. Decade after decade politicians have been spending America into debt, leaving an IOU to be paid by future generations—our children and grandchildren. If you visit USDebtClock.org, you will see the debt dials spinning at a dizzying pace as the US government adds more than a million dollars worth of debt *every forty seconds*. As I write these words, the national debt has passed thirty trillion dollars, nearly a quarter of a million dollars for every American taxpayer.

This soaring level of debt is unsustainable, and at some point the US economic system will collapse. This is not scare talk. This is a self-evident fact. Economist Herbert Stein (1916–1999), a former chairman of the Council of Economic Advisers under presidents Nixon and Ford, once said (and this statement has become known as Stein's Law), "If something cannot go on forever, it will stop." The soaring national debt cannot go on forever—and when it stops, when the US government can no longer pay the interest on its debt, it will collapse the global economy.[21]

There's a scene in Ernest Hemingway's novel *The Sun Also Rises* in which two characters, Mike and Bill, are discussing Mike's impoverished condition. Bill asks, "How did you go bankrupt?"

Mike replies, "Two ways. Gradually and then suddenly."[22]

My friend, that is how America is going bankrupt. It is happening quite gradually—for now. But the national debt is headed for a tipping point—a point when we can no longer sustain a welfare state, a national defense, or an entitlement system. Then the collapse will happen suddenly—and catastrophically. If something cannot go on forever, it *will* stop.

AND NOW THE GOOD NEWS..

In view of all these catastrophes looming on our horizon, you may be asking, "Is there any hope?" My answer to you is a resounding yes! Our hope is in the nail-scarred hands of Jesus.

Is your faith firmly anchored in the Lord Jesus Christ? If it is, then none of the dire events and circumstances I've described to you can shake your confidence or fill you with fear. As a believer and follower of the Lord, you can be certain that

- this world we live in will one day come to an end,

- this world is *not* our ultimate home,

- we are temporarily visiting this planet and our assignment from God is to share Christ and save as many people as our sovereign Lord will allow,

- one day the Lord Jesus Christ will return to take us home to heaven,

- the Lord Himself gave us certain signs in Matthew 24 to alert us to the approaching last days, and

- those who truly love and follow the Lord Jesus long for His return.

Further, the knowledge that He is returning soon should motivate us to witness, serve, and give to the cause of spreading His gospel.

In view of these truths, there is no greater test of the

genuineness of our faith than our preparedness for His return. That preparedness should be on full display in the way we live our lives each day. We must have our spiritual luggage packed and ready for our departure from this planet. We must be busy serving God so that it makes no difference whether we leave this life today or decades hence.

I once heard about a country preacher who held a tent revival meeting. One night he decided to gauge the spiritual readiness of his audience members. He wanted to see if their faith was genuine. So he arranged to have a young man with a trumpet on the roof of a nearby building.

During the service he asked his audience, "How many of you are ready to meet the Lord Jesus in the air if He were to return right now?"

Every hand went up.

The preacher asked a second time, "If the last trumpet were to sound right now, would you be ready to meet the Lord?"

This time most hands went up—but not all of them.

The preacher nodded to a man in the back of the tent, who quietly slipped out to signal the man with the trumpet.

Moments later the mighty trumpet blasted outside the tent—and more than half of the panic-stricken audience members dived under their chairs to hide themselves from the face of Jesus.

Are you ready for the second coming of Jesus Christ?

Your preparedness for His return is the clearest sign of the genuineness of your faith.

As believers we don't view the end of history with alarm but with *hope*, knowing that Jesus is returning and God controls the future. I believe we are witnessing events that the Bible foretold regarding the end-time—events that Jesus foretold in Matthew 24 and 25.

In the coming chapters we will peer into the future through the words of the Lord Jesus Himself. Let's hear what He has to say about the end of civilization and the coming of the one world ruler.

Chapter 2

THE LABOR PAINS OF HISTORY

Pastor Andrew Brunson has been a missionary to Turkey since the mid-1990s. In 2016 he served as the pastor of a small Turkish congregation, Izmir Dirilis (Resurrection) Church. After a coup d'état attempt against Turkish leader Recep Tayyip Erdoğan, many people were swept up in a massive wave of arrests—including Pastor Brunson. He was falsely accused of involvement in the coup attempt. In October 2018, thanks to the prayers of many Christians and strong diplomatic pressure from the US government, Pastor Brunson was released.

Glad to be free, Pastor Brunson returned to the United States. He was shocked to discover how much America had changed while he was in a Turkish prison.

He discovered that American government officials had begun to attack the religious liberty of Christians in the United States. For example, Colorado officials sued a Christian baker to force him to make cakes for same-sex weddings. Washington state sued a Christian florist to force her to create floral arrangements for gay weddings. Pennsylvania and California sued a Catholic charity, the Little Sisters of the Poor, to force the nuns to pay for abortion-inducing contraceptives.[1]

After seeing how much America had changed during his absence, Pastor Brunson said, "I was isolated for a few years, and coming back to the states was almost like coming back to a different country....We in the West have not experienced [persecution] very much... but I think we are going to. I think it's coming to this country."[2]

The world has always hated Jesus and His gospel. Today more than ever that hatred is out in the open. It is displayed by government officials toward Christians who simply want to follow their conscience and practice their faith. If you witness, if you share the good news of Jesus Christ in your neighborhood, at your workplace, or on campus, if you try to conduct your life according to your Christian moral values, you can expect increasing hostility and persecution.

Jesus said one of the signs that He is coming soon is the sign of growing persecution: "Then you will be handed over to be persecuted and put to death, and you will be hated by all nations because of me" (Matt.

24:9). Every attack and insult you suffer for the Lord's sake is a signpost that points to the imminent return of Jesus Christ.

WHAT JESUS TAUGHT ABOUT THE END-TIME

Ever since Jesus walked the dusty roads of Palestine, His followers have been asking, "Are we approaching the end-time? When will the Lord Jesus return?" His disciples were as curious about the end-time as we are today. And Jesus had much to say about the closing days of human history.

We must go to the disciples' questions and our Lord's replies to answer these questions. In Matthew 24 we find the Lord's answer to His disciples on Mount Olivet (or the Mount of Olives), in a sermon known as the Olivet Discourse:

> Jesus left the temple and was walking away when his disciples came up to him to call his attention to its buildings. "Do you see all these things?" he asked. "Truly I tell you, not one stone here will be left on another; every one will be thrown down."
>
> As Jesus was sitting on the Mount of Olives, the disciples came to him privately. "Tell us," they said, "when will this happen, and what will be the sign of your coming and of the end of the age?"
>
> Jesus answered: "Watch out that no one deceives you. For many will come in my name,

claiming, 'I am the Messiah,' and will deceive many. You will hear of wars and rumors of wars, but see to it that you are not alarmed. Such things must happen, but the end is still to come. Nation will rise against nation, and kingdom against kingdom. There will be famines and earthquakes in various places. All these are the beginning of birth pains.

"Then you will be handed over to be persecuted and put to death, and you will be hated by all nations because of me. At that time many will turn away from the faith and will betray and hate each other, and many false prophets will appear and deceive many people. Because of the increase of wickedness, the love of most will grow cold, but the one who stands firm to the end will be saved. And this gospel of the kingdom will be preached in the whole world as a testimony to all nations, and then the end will come."

—MATTHEW 24:1–14

Jesus and His disciples sat atop the Mount of Olives, which took its name from the many olive trees that once covered its slopes. The Mount of Olives served as a Jewish cemetery a thousand years before Christ, and roughly one hundred fifty thousand graves dot its slopes. From the top of the Mount of Olives, Jesus and His disciples had a clear view of the Temple Mount in Jerusalem.

The disciples asked, "When will this [the destruction

of the Temple in Jerusalem] happen, and what will be the sign of your coming and of the end of the age?"

In this one sentence the disciples asked two questions: (1) When will the Temple be destroyed as Jesus predicted? (2) What will be the sign by which we may recognize the coming of the Messiah and the end of history? It's a short question, but Jesus' reply is the longest answer to any question in the Bible. This reply takes up two chapters, Matthew 24 and 25. The Lord's reply is rightly called a discourse (sermon), and it is the second-longest sermon of Jesus recorded in the Bible. (The longest, of course, is the Sermon on the Mount, in Matthew 5–7).

THE QUESTIONS AND EXPECTATIONS OF THE DISCIPLES

The words of Jesus in the Olivet Discourse are so relevant to our times that I felt a strong sense of urgency in writing this book. Now more than ever, we who follow Jesus need to understand the Lord's prophecy. If we truly want to understand the signs of the end-time, we must carefully study this prophecy from the lips of Jesus Himself.

Let's begin with the background of the disciples and the question they asked. All of Jesus' disciples were schooled in the Jewish traditions. They had been taught that Messiah would come and rule the earth, liberating the Jewish people from oppression by foreign powers.

The Jewish nation had suffered tyranny and persecution repeatedly through history. Israel had been enslaved in Egypt, attacked by the pagan Canaanite nations, enslaved again by the Assyrians and the Babylonians, and conquered by the Romans.

So the Jewish people found hope in the teachings of Isaiah 11, about the root of Jesse, who would bear "the Spirit of the knowledge and fear of the LORD," who would "slay the wicked" with the breath of His mouth, who would gather "the surviving remnant of his people" to Himself (vv. 2, 4, 11). They took comfort from Isaiah 9:6, which promised, "For to us a child is born, to us a son is given, and the government will be on his shoulders."

They clung to God's pledge in Jeremiah 23:5–6: "'The days are coming,' declares the LORD, 'when I will raise up for David a righteous Branch, a King who will reign wisely and do what is just and right in the land. In his days Judah will be saved and Israel will live in safety. This is the name by which he will be called: The LORD Our Righteous Savior.'"

These promises of the coming Messiah were in the minds of the disciples as they questioned Jesus. They knew that Jesus was born of the line of David, the son of Jesse. They knew that Jesus was supernaturally conceived and born of a virgin. They had seen Him perform supernatural healings, miracles, and signs. He had promised to rise from the dead, so they expected Him to announce the beginning of His global rule at any moment.

The disciples asked essentially the same question

both before and after the resurrection. In Acts 1:6 they gathered around and asked, "Lord, are you at this time going to restore the kingdom to Israel?"

The Jews of that time believed that the Messiah would come only once—and they believed that when the Messiah came, He would do everything that was prophesied about Him. He would demonstrate His power over death and declare His global rule.

Before and after the resurrection, it was natural for the disciples to wonder, "When are You going to make the announcement? When are You going to end our oppression and restore the kingdom to Israel?" It didn't occur to them that Jesus would come to earth, live, die, rise from the dead, and then leave the earth for hundreds of years before returning to fulfill the Old Testament prophecies. They thought that all the Messianic prophecies referred to a single event—the coming of the Messiah to reign on earth.

The disciples were certain that Jesus' next move would be the subjugation of the enemy nations. They expected to share in the power, wealth, and prestige of His reign, and they thought He was only days away from establishing His kingdom.

THE LABOR PAINS OF HISTORY

Matthew 24 tells us that Jesus and the disciples visited the great temple of Jerusalem before going out to the Mount of Olives. In verses 1–2 Matthew writes, "Jesus left the temple and was walking away when His disciples came up to Him to call His attention to its buildings. 'Do you see all these things?' he asked. 'Truly I tell you, not one stone here will be left on another; every one will be thrown down.'"

Why did they call His attention to the temple buildings? Perhaps they were marveling at this seemingly indestructible edifice, built sturdily enough to stand for a thousand years. Yet Jesus told them the temple would be razed to the ground. His words must have seemed unthinkable to the disciples. A mere forty years later, however, the temple would be leveled exactly as Jesus foretold.

During Passover in April of AD 70, the Roman general (and future emperor) Titus laid siege to Jerusalem. Jews who tried to escape were captured and crucified outside the city walls, as many as five hundred per day. The Romans starved the inhabitants of Jerusalem, and the bodies of those who died of starvation were stacked up in the valleys of Kidron and Hinnom. Roman siege towers shattered the city walls. On August 10 the Romans set fire to the temple and took six thousand women and children prisoner in the temple courtyard. Then the Romans sacrificed to their pagan gods, profaning the altar in the holy of holies.[3]

By the time the Romans had completed their frenzy of destruction, the Jerusalem temple was destroyed, just as Jesus had predicted. Today archaeologists can scarcely identify any stones as having belonged to the temple of Jesus' day. As archaeologist Harry Thomas

Frank observed, "Strictly speaking, the Temple proper is not a matter of archaeological consideration since only one stone from it and parts of another can be positively identified."[4] The Lord's prophecy was completely fulfilled. Not one stone was left standing on another.

The disciples must have been baffled by Jesus' prediction about the temple. Matthew doesn't record any further dialogue between Jesus and the disciples until they had gone out of the city and ascended the Mount of Olives. Perhaps the disciples were so dumbstruck by the Lord's prediction that they followed Jesus in silence to the Mount of Olives.

When they reached the summit, the disciples asked, "When will this [the destruction of the Temple] happen, and what will be the sign of your coming and of the end of the age?"

In verse 4 Jesus begins His lengthy answer, the Olivet Discourse. He gives the disciples several indications that His visible Messianic rule will not take place soon, but rather in the distant future. He says the first signs will be like labor pains. During these labor pains there will sometimes be false alarms, including false messiahs. There will be international warfare. There will be famine. There will be earthquakes.

But this is only the *beginning* of the labor pains. The baby's arrival is still in the future.

Now, to any men reading this book I have a word of advice: I urge you to never, never, *never* say aloud that you have experienced anything remotely similar to labor pain. Even if you have suffered from kidney stones or gallstones, you have never experienced anything like the labor pains of a woman.

At what point in the nine-month gestation period do labor pains occur? Not during conception. Not during the middle of the pregnancy. No; labor pains occur in the *late stages* of pregnancy, shortly before childbirth. And they occur with increasing frequency and intensity until the baby is born. Jesus uses the metaphor of labor pains to tell us that the events associated with His return will intensify shortly before His return.

FIRST LABOR PAIN: FALSEHOOD AND DECEPTION

Jesus names six "labor pains," six signs that foreshadow the conclusion of history. Each of these six signs has always been with us. The difference is that, like labor pains, they will become more frequent and more severe until Jesus appears.

The first of the six signs is widespread falsehood and deception. Verses 4 and 5 say: "Jesus answered: 'Watch out that no one deceives you. For many will come in my name, claiming, "I am the Messiah," and will deceive many.'" We see this happening already. Waves of deceivers have brought false, unbiblical "gospels" into the church, deceiving many.

These false gospels include the prosperity gospel, the social gospel, the progressive gospel, the "love wins" gospel, and more. Some pastors mutilate the Bible, leaving out the parts they dislike, whether it's

Old Testament history or the New Testament warnings about hell or the passages about sexual purity. They major on some of Jesus' teachings and ignore others. Some, I'm saddened to say, preach Marxism under the guise of "compassion" or "progressive Christianity." Just a few years ago I would not have believed this was possible; today it is rampant in so-called evangelical churches.

(My 2020 book *Saving Christianity?* offers an in-depth examination of the heresy and falsehood infecting the evangelical church.)

Jesus warns His disciples—and He warns you and me: Keep your eyes open. Beware of false teachers and deceptive "gospels." Don't be deceived.

I fear for the church in these days. As the number of deceivers grows, so does the number of vulnerable people. Many are desperately seeking answers for the calamities and unrest that threaten the globe. I fear they will fall prey to the glib, deceitful answers offered by false teachers.

As we see unparalleled wickedness and immorality in the church, as we see good condemned as evil and evil exalted as good, as lifestyles of sin are being baptized in the church—we must stand firm. We must not compromise. We must not give in to false teaching. Stand firm on God's truth.

Second Labor Pain: Wars and Rumors of Wars

The second of the six labor pains is wars and rumors of wars. The world today is a roiling cauldron of international tensions. Following the United States' humiliating exit from Afghanistan, war rages between the Taliban and the Islamic State. Civil war rages in Yemen, Somalia, the Maghreb, Sudan, and other parts of Africa. Ethiopian, Eritrean, and Sudanese forces clash. The Islamic State insurgency threatens Iraq's stability, and the Boko Haram insurgency threatens Nigeria.

The Syrian Civil War continues year after year. Israel-Palestinian tensions frequently flare up into open warfare. Russia besieges Ukraine. China threatens Taiwan. Iran is developing an "Islamic bomb" and announcing plans to destroy Israel. Murderous drug wars rage in Mexico, Colombia, and Venezuela.

The greatest threat to global stability is Communist China—the nation that unleashed the deadly COVID-19 pandemic on the world. That pandemic—almost certainly caused by careless handling of dangerously enhanced viruses at a research lab in Wuhan—killed 6 million people worldwide by the end of 2021 (according to *official* reports; estimates by the Institute for Health Metrics and Evaluation suggest the *actual* global death toll exceeds 15.5 million).[5] The pandemic has killed more Americans than all Americans killed in World War II.[6]

In any discussion of Bible prophecy, China rarely

receives the attention it deserves. Though the word China does not appear in the Bible, it is clear that China figures prominently in Bible prophecy. Daniel 11 tells us that the Antichrist will be alarmed by "reports from the east" and go off to war (v. 44). Revelation 9 describes the great final war, in which an army from the east, numbering "twice ten thousand times ten thousand" soldiers (that is, two hundred million), crosses into the Holy Land (v. 16). Currently there is only one army of that size in the world: Communist China's People's Liberation Army, with 2.185 million soldiers in uniform.[7]

THE COMMUNIST DEBT TRAP

China has become the global neighborhood bully. Through its "Belt and Road Initiative," China uses its wealth and influence to build infrastructure in nations around the world, placing those nations deep in debt. Being in debt to Communist China is like being in debt to the Mafia. When China decides to call the debt, the debtor nation must do China's bidding. In this way, China is building a globe-circling military and economic empire to challenge the United States and other Western nations for world domination.

China is asserting its bullying influence throughout Asia, the Middle East, and Africa. For example, from 2009 to 2014, China upgraded the deep water port of Bata in Equatorial Guinea on the west coast of central Africa through its China Road & Bridge Co. In 2019 the United States discovered that China was engaged in turning the commercial port of Bata into a Chinese military base.[8] Similarly, in the east-central African nation of Uganda, China is poised to take control of Entebbe International Airport as a result of Uganda's inability to repay a loan from China's Export-Import Bank.[9] This will give China a potential military air base in that mineral-rich African nation.

Communist China has lent staggering amounts of cash to countries around the world—loans totaling more than 5 percent of the world's gross domestic product, more than the lending of the World Bank, the International Monetary Fund, and the Organization for Economic Cooperation and Development *combined*. As a result, China now controls the electrical grid of Laos as well as the gold and silver mines of Tajikistan. China debt-trapped Sri Lanka and Pakistan into ceding control of their busiest seaports—along with the revenues from those ports.[10]

China has also been infiltrating American corporations and universities. Through its Thousand Talents Program, China recruits highly placed Americans to spy and steal technology. Through its Confucius Institutes, China indoctrinates American high school and college students in the glories of Communism.

The Chinese Communists also work with "woke" activist groups (including Black Lives Matter and Antifa) to promote Communism in America. By amplifying anti-American claims of "systemic racism,"

China boasts that it is morally superior to America even while committing unthinkable atrocities against its own people. A video produced by the state-owned China Global Television Network uses critical race theory to lecture Americans about "being anti-racist." Meanwhile, China confines its own Uyghur minorities in concentration camps, forcing them to pick cotton as slaves—practices America fought a Civil War to abolish.[11]

FUNDING ARMAGEDDON

American companies, including Apple, Nike, NBCUniversal, and Disney, have turned a blind eye to China's human rights abuses in order to exploit China's sweatshop economy. These companies profit enormously—but they inevitably come under the thumb of their Communist overlords. Following are some examples.

Disney has invested billions of dollars in two theme parks in Communist China—Shanghai Disney Resort and Hong Kong Disneyland. According to the BBC, Shanghai Disney Resort welcomes Communist Party cells on its property and happily reports that "really good ideas come from the [Communist] Party committee."[12] Disney's 2020 film *Mulan* was partially filmed in Xinjiang, where Communist slave camps imprison Uyghurs, Tibetans, Christians, and other minorities for "counter-revolutionary thought." In *Mulan*'s credits the producers thank the Xinjiang Public Security Bureau, which operates the concentration camps.[13] If Disney-owned ABC News seems shockingly pro-China these days, you now know why.

NBCUniversal has invested billions in its Universal Beijing theme park and resort. In February 2022 NBC broadcast the Beijing Winter Olympics, which human rights observers have condemned as "the Genocide Olympics" because of China's enslavement of two million Uyghur Muslims. (Strangely, there's hardly a word of complaint from Muslim nations—I know because I read the Arabic press.)

Nike states boldly that "Nike is a brand that is of China and for China," adding that the company "does not source products from the [Xinjiang Uyghur Autonomous Region], and we have confirmed with our contract suppliers that they are not using textiles or spun yarn from the region."[14] Nike is fully supportive of the brutal Chinese Communist regime but claims that at least no slave labor is involved in making Nike shoes.

Turkish-American basketball star Enes Kanter of the Boston Celtics doesn't believe Nike. Kanter wears custom shoes bearing the anti-Nike slogans "Modern Day Slavery" and "No More Excuses." Kanter told an interviewer, "Every time you put those [Nike] shoes on your feet, or you put that T-shirt on your back, there are so many tears and so much oppression and so much blood behind it all."[15]

Apple manufactures almost all of its products in

Communist China—and earns 20 percent of its income in China. In May 2021 the *New York Times* observed that Apple CEO Tim Cook pioneered Apple's entry into China—and now China has Apple over a barrel. "Just as Mr. Cook figured out how to make China work for Apple," the *Times* said, "China is making Apple work for the Chinese government."[16] Laborers in Apple factories earn $3.15 per hour, live in prisonlike dormitories, and work eleven hours a day, six days a week.[17]

These and many other American companies have been wooed to China by cheap sweatshop labor. They are enriching the oppressive Chinese Communist government and building up the People's Liberation Army. Apple, Nike, NBCUniversal, and Disney are just a few among many American companies that are helping to fund the coming Armageddon.

Do Not Be Alarmed

In November 2021 John Mearsheimer, a political science professor at the University of Chicago, appeared on the PBS *NewsHour* to discuss the future of US-China relations. President Biden had just held a teleconference with China's Communist leader Xi Jinping. *NewsHour* host Nick Schifrin asked Mearsheimer, "Do you believe the meeting served US interests?"

Mearsheimer replied, "No, I don't think so," adding that Mr. Biden's goal was "to dampen down the intense security competition that exists now between China and the United States....My argument is, it's impossible to achieve that goal. The fact is that the United States and China are destined to engage in a serious security competition, in effect, another Cold War, for the foreseeable future.

"And the reason for that is very simple. China is bent on dominating Asia. It's bent on controlling the South China Sea, taking back Taiwan, and dominating the East China Sea. The United States has no intention of allowing China to achieve any one of those three goals....The end result is, we're going to be in each other's face for the foreseeable future, and we're going to live in a very dangerous world in east Asia."[18]

US-China conflict appears inevitable. As Jesus said, "You will hear of wars and rumors of wars, but see to it that you are not alarmed. Such things must happen, but the end is still to come. Nation will rise against nation, and kingdom against kingdom." From Israel to Africa to Afghanistan to East Asia, we hear of wars and rumors of war. Nations are challenging nations. "All these," Jesus said, "are the beginning of birth pains."

How should we respond to a world in which the risk of war increases daily? Jesus tells us, "See to it that you are not alarmed." In other words, take heart! Be courageous and full of faith! And remember, as Jesus said, "Such things must happen, but the end is still to come."

It's instructive that Jesus says, "Nation will rise against nation, and kingdom against kingdom." The original Greek word translated "nation" is *ethnos*, a word used to indicate an ethnic or tribal multitude, a Gentile populace or country. The original Greek word translated "kingdom" is *basileia*, which refers to a royal power, a dominion ruled by a single authoritarian monarch or dictator.

At the time Jesus spoke these words, every nation in the known world was a kingdom or empire (*basileia*). But there had been nations in the past that were not kingdoms but democracies (*ethnos*). The Athenian democracy was established in 508 BC and lasted for nearly two centuries before it fell in 322 BC. Rome had also been a democratic republic at one time. Established in 509 BC, the Roman Republic ended in 27 BC with the establishment of the Roman Empire.

So it's possible that when Jesus spoke of "nations," *ethnos*, He might have been referring to democratic countries—or He might have been referring to ethnic groups. In other words, He might have been prophesying about coming *racial* strife. In many nations around the world—in the Middle East, in Africa, in the Baltic region, in many parts of Asia, we have seen racial violence and "ethnic cleansing" destroying countless lives. In the United States, we see activists, radical politicians, and cable news talking heads trying to stir up a race war in America.

Jesus is telling us that many nations and ethnic groups will increasingly clash and war against each other before His return. There will be wars and rumors of war.

THIRD LABOR PAIN: FAMINE AND EARTHQUAKE

Next, in Matthew 24:7–8 our Lord reveals the third labor pain: "There will be famines and earthquakes in various places. All these are the beginning of birth pains." In the parallel account in Luke 21:11 Jesus says, "There will be great earthquakes, famines and pestilences in various places, and fearful events and great signs from heaven." In other words, there will be natural catastrophes of staggering proportions, including plagues and terror and signs in the heavens.

You undoubtedly recall how at the beginning of the pandemic, in 2020, people began to panic buy and soon store shelves were empty of hand sanitizer, canned soup, and toilet paper (which some people called "white gold"). In the days that Jesus describes here, there will be panic and terror on an unimaginable scale, making the pandemic era seem like a utopia.

When Jesus says, "There will be famines and earthquakes in various places," He means in many places at the same time, all over the world. John, in the Book of Revelation, experiences a vision of that time and he describes it using the imagery of a scroll with a series of seals that are broken, one after the other. The breaking of the sixth seal causes the stars to fall from heaven. The breaking of the seventh seal causes the crops and the vegetation to be devastated.

Yet as terrifying as these signs are, Jesus reminds us

that this is not yet the end of history. "All these," He says, "are the *beginning* of birth pains."

FOURTH LABOR PAIN: BELIEVERS WILL BE HATED

In Matthew 24:9 Jesus reveals the fourth labor pain: believers will be hated because they proclaim the name of Jesus: "Then you will be handed over to be persecuted and put to death, and you will be hated by all nations because of me."

Please understand, when the world hates us and persecutes us, all that rage is not directed against us. The world is raging against God. When the resurrected Lord Jesus appeared to Saul of Tarsus on the road to Damascus, He did not say, "Why are you persecuting My people?" Jesus said, "Why are you persecuting *Me*?" Don't take persecution personally. Instead, count it an honor to suffer for the sake of Jesus.

Persecution takes many forms. In many countries, the government makes it hard for churches to obtain permits for constructing or repairing churches. Persecution may include discrimination against Christians who are seeking a job or legal representation. Many countries, especially Muslim countries, ban Christian evangelism and arrest Christian missionaries. In Communist China, Saudi Arabia, and other anti-Christian countries, believers must worship in secret—and authorities often raid house churches and arrest everyone who attends. In many parts of the world, Christians are beaten or killed, and churches are destroyed.

Christians have had to flee areas controlled by Islamic groups like ISIS, Al-Qaeda, Al-Shabaab, Boko Haram, and the Hausa-Fulani militants. These groups engage in mass murder, kidnappings, rape, and the destruction of entire villages.

One of the most vicious and brutal persecutors of the church in our time is the Communist North Korean regime of Kim Jong-un. The government has outlawed the Christian faith in any form, from individual prayer to owning a Bible to meeting together for Christian worship. Christians who practice their faith risk imprisonment in a concentration camp, torture, and death.

The Chinese Communist Party has stepped up its persecution of the Chinese Christian church. The government bans anyone under the age of eighteen from attending church. Police have raided house churches, destroyed church property, and burned Bibles. The government has also forced churches to install cameras so that state officials, using facial recognition technology, can identify and track Chinese Christians. The Communist Party hates Christianity and fears China's estimated one hundred million Christians.[19]

FIFTH LABOR PAIN: APOSTASY

In verses 10–13 Jesus describes the fifth labor pain, apostasy, which comes as a direct result of the fourth labor pain, persecution. As persecution intensifies around the world, many will forsake Christ and join the nonbelievers. Jesus said: "At that time many will turn away from the faith and will betray and hate each other, and many false prophets will appear and deceive many people. Because of the increase of wickedness, the love of most will grow cold, but the one who stands firm to the end will be saved."

People will defect from the faith for three principal reasons.

First, they will defect because the price of following Jesus is too high. They will decide they do not want to pay the cost of discipleship.

Second, they will defect because false teachers will arise with deceptive but persuasive messages. These false teachers will speak from church pulpits. They will write best-selling books and appear on TV. They will have the most popular social media accounts. They'll use variations on the same lies Satan used in the Garden of Eden: "Did God really say...?" and "You shall be like God."

Third, they will defect because sin is attractive and seductive. Jesus said, "Enter through the narrow gate. For wide is the gate and broad is the road that leads to destruction, and many enter through it. But small is the gate and narrow the road that leads to life, and only a few find it" (Matt. 7:13–14). The wide gate is the gate of selfishness and the temporary pleasures of sin. The narrow gate is the gate of righteousness and everlasting pleasures in heaven.

There are many in the church today who are what I call "hangers on." They may outwardly look like believers, but they are not truly born-again. They are members of the institutional, visible church but have never joined Christ's invisible church. Because of the increase of wickedness, the love of those "hangers on" will grow cold, and they will fall away from the faith.

But genuine believers who stand firm to the end will be saved.

Sixth Labor Pain: Global Evangelization

In Matthew 24:14 Jesus describes the sixth and final labor pain: "And this gospel of the kingdom will be preached in the whole world as a testimony to all nations, and then the end will come." The final birth pain is that the gospel of Jesus Christ will be preached to the farthest, most inaccessible corners of the globe. Many believers in Communist China and North Korea, in the Middle East and Africa and Asia are standing firm against threats and persecution. They are spreading the gospel, even though witnessing for Jesus is a crime punishable by death.

Their joy is unspeakable; their faith is unquenchable; their hearts are unafraid. While false believers in the West spread fake gospels and defect from the truth, these true believers around the world are joyfully paying the cost of following Jesus.

That is why our Leading The Way ministry is thrilled to have a part in encouraging these believers and spreading the good news of Jesus Christ to the far corners of the earth. The final labor pain of human history is that the gospel of the kingdom of God shall be preached as a witness to all nations—and then, Jesus says, the end will come!

Come, Lord Jesus!

Chapter 3

"THOSE DAYS" AND "THAT DAY"

HE COVID-19 PANDEMIC is an event most of us would like to forget. Tragically many people reading this book have lost loved ones, lost their health, lost their business or their job, or suffered in other ways from this global catastrophe.

It began in late 2019, when a cluster of hospital patients in Wuhan, China, exhibited pneumonia-like symptoms and fever due to a mysterious and unknown ailment. Within months, the virus known as COVID-19 had spread around the world. By the end of 2021 the virus had taken millions of lives worldwide and had cost the world more than ten trillion dollars in lost economic production alone, according to projections by *The Economist*.[1]

Month after month, throughout the pandemic, the number one topic of conversation was, "When will we get back to normal?" or, "I can't wait until life gets back to normal!" or even, "What if we *never* get back to normal?"

In March 2020, as the United States began locking down, readers of the *MIT Technology Review* were stunned to open an article titled "We're Not Going Back to Normal." The article began with these words: "We all want things to go back to normal quickly. But what most of us have probably not yet realized—yet will soon—is that things won't go back to normal after a few weeks, or even a few months. Some things never will."[2]

As human beings we long for normalcy, security, and peace. We long for social stability, economic stability, a sense that our jobs and our lives are dependable and secure. Invisible viruses, rioting and unrest, inflation and recession, wars and rumors of wars—all these threats make us anxious and fearful. These are normal emotions in the face of such disturbing news.

Yet the realistic message of God's Word is that times of peace and tranquility are merely temporary respites from the troubles of this life. We live in a world that is broken by sin. The only permanent peace this world will ever know is that future time when Jesus, the Prince of Peace, comes to rule for all eternity.

But before the eternal reign of Jesus begins, the world must pass through a time of unprecedented terrors and sufferings. In Matthew 24:21 Jesus tells us, "For then there will be great distress, unequaled from the beginning of the world until now—and never to be equaled again." For unbelievers, this will be a time of absolute despair, but for those who trust in Jesus, these events will be a sign of hope, signaling that Jesus will soon come to take us to heaven.

Two Events, Centuries Apart

Jesus said that no one but God knows when that day will come. It could be today or a thousand years from now. Only the Father knows the precise timetable of the end-time.

Listen as Jesus continues the Olivet Discourse:

> So when you see standing in the holy place "the abomination that causes desolation," spoken of through the prophet Daniel—let the reader understand—then let those who are in Judea flee to the mountains. Let no one on the housetop go down to take anything out of the house. Let no one in the field go back to get their cloak. How dreadful it will be in those days for pregnant women and nursing mothers! Pray that your flight will not take place in winter or on the Sabbath. For then there will be great distress, unequaled from the beginning of the world until now—and never to be equaled again.
>
> If those days had not been cut short, no one would survive, but for the sake of the elect those

days will be shortened. At that time if anyone says to you, "Look, here is the Messiah!" or, "There he is!" do not believe it. For false messiahs and false prophets will appear and perform great signs and wonders to deceive, if possible, even the elect. See, I have told you ahead of time.

So if anyone tells you, "There he is, out in the wilderness," do not go out; or, "Here he is, in the inner rooms," do not believe it. For as lightning that comes from the east is visible even in the west, so will be the coming of the Son of Man. Wherever there is a carcass, there the vultures will gather.

—MATTHEW 24:15–28

In this passage, Jesus speaks of two events. First, He tells His disciples about an event that will take place in AD 70—forty years after His ascension into heaven— the destruction of Jerusalem by the Romans.

Second, He tells them what is going to take place immediately before His return.

How do we know He is speaking of two separated events? We know because of the words Jesus uses—a difference in wording that is clear in the original Greek but is sometimes obscured in our English translations. In this passage, Jesus tells us what will happen in "those days" (*ekeinos hēmera*) forty years in the future— and what will happen "on that day" (*tote*) when Jesus returns in triumph.

He says (verses 19 and 22), "How dreadful it will

be in *those days* for pregnant women and nursing mothers!...If *those days* had not been cut short, no one would survive, but for the sake of the elect *those days* will be shortened" (emphasis added).

He also says (vv. 21 and 23), "For then [*tote*, meaning "on that day"] there will be great distress, unequaled from the beginning of the world until now—and never to be equaled again....At that time [*tote*] if anyone says to you, 'Look, here is the Messiah!' or, 'There he is!' do not believe it."

Though these two widely separated events seem woven into one message, you can tell which event Jesus is speaking of by separating "those days" from "that day."

WHAT LIES AHEAD

The terrifying future event Jesus speaks of is known as the great tribulation. The return of the Lord Jesus to take His church away from the earth is known as the rapture. The theological term *rapture* derives from the Greek word *harpazō*, meaning "to snatch away suddenly." Paul used this word when he said in 1 Thessalonians 4:16–17 that "the Lord himself will come down from heaven, with a loud command, with the voice of the archangel and with the trumpet call of God, and the dead in Christ will rise first. After that, we who are still alive and are left *will be caught up* (*harpazō*) together with them in the clouds" (emphasis added).

There are essentially three theological positions regarding when Jesus will return to "rapture" His church. Many great and godly Bible teachers hold differing positions on this question. The three positions are:

1. *Pre-tribulation*. Jesus will take His church out of the world *before* the great tribulation begins.

2. *Mid-tribulation*. The church will go through the first half of the great tribulation—then Jesus will return and "rapture" His followers.

3. *Post-tribulation*. The church will go through the entire great tribulation, and at the end of that time, Jesus will return to "rapture" the church.

You are free to choose the position that makes the most sense to you, as you understand God's Word. You will not lose your salvation for choosing the "wrong" position on God's timing of the rapture.

Which of these three positions do I hold? Well, let me tell you a story about that.

Back in 1980 a friend and I were discussing this question over breakfast. I asked his position on the rapture, and he replied with a shrug. He asked my position, and I gave the same reply. So we decided we both needed to stake out a fourth position. We even came up with a label for our theological perspective: "Pan-tribulationist." Simply put, we had decided to wait and see how the tribulation would "pan out."

I wish I could assure you that the church will never have to go through the great tribulation—but I simply don't know that to be true. I agree with the English astronomer-mathematician Sir Isaac Newton (1643–1727), who wrote that God gave us Bible prophecies "not to gratify men's curiosities by enabling them to foreknow things, but that after they were fulfilled they might be interpreted by the event, and his own Providence, not the Interpreters, be then manifested thereby to the world."[3] In other words, Sir Isaac Newton was also content to wait and see how the prophecies of the Bible would "pan out."

So, as far as I know from my study of Scripture, it is possible that the church may have to go through some or all of the great tribulation. Because of this possibility, I believe with all my heart—the heart of a pastor, a father, and a grandfather—that we should prepare our children for any eventuality that may come. We must train our children to be full of faith and courage. We need to speak honestly to them about the troubled days that almost certainly lie ahead.

THE ABOMINATION OF DESOLATION

Jesus said, "So when you see standing in the holy place 'the abomination that causes desolation,' spoken of through the prophet Daniel—let the reader understand—then let those who are in Judea flee to the mountains." What is this "abomination that causes desolation" that the prophet Daniel spoke about?

In Daniel 9:27 the angel Gabriel tells Daniel that a future ruler will "confirm a covenant with many for one 'seven.' In the middle of the 'seven' he will put an end to sacrifice and offering. And at the temple he will set up an abomination that causes desolation, until the end that is decreed is poured out on him." Gabriel also speaks of the "abomination that causes desolation" in Daniel 11:31 and 12:11.

Like many Bible prophecies, this prophecy in Daniel has two interpretations, two fulfillments. First, the "abomination that causes desolation" refers to an incident in Jewish history under King Antiochus IV Epiphanes. Antiochus was a Greek king who reigned over the Seleucid Empire (including Palestine) from 175 BC until his death in 164 BC. He called himself "the magnificent god," but his enemies called him "the madman" or "the insane one." As an act of desecration, an insult to the God of Israel, he slaughtered pigs on the sacred altar and, by some accounts, forced the Jewish priests to eat it. He also set up an idol of the Greek god Zeus in the temple—the "abomination that causes desolation." He slaughtered thousands of Jewish men and sold their women and children into slavery.

All of this took place in fulfillment of the prophecy of Gabriel to Daniel—and it happened two hundred years before Jesus spoke to His disciples on the Mount of Olives. If the "abomination that causes desolation" of Antiochus Epiphanes had already taken place two centuries earlier, why did Jesus speak of the "abomination that causes desolation" as a *future* event? It's because there are two interpretations, two fulfillments, of this one prophecy in Daniel.

There are also two valid ways of interpreting the Lord's prophecy regarding the "abomination that causes desolation":

1. You can take this as a prophecy that will be fulfilled in a literal, physical way.

You can interpret it to mean that, when the Antichrist arises, he will physically reconstruct the temple in Jerusalem. Orthodox Jewish tradition holds that the third and final temple will be built on the original site when Messiah comes.

But there's a problem: the Temple Mount is dominated by structures that are holy to Muslims—the al-Aqsa Mosque, the Dome of the Rock, and the Dome of the Chain, plus four minarets. The Dome of the Rock is built around a rock that Muslims believe was the place where Muhammad began a night journey into heaven. To rebuild the temple on its original site, some or all of these Islamic holy sites would have to be destroyed. Can you imagine how the Muslim world would react to that? Of course, nothing is impossible with God, so the Lord's Olivet prophecy could be fulfilled in a literal, physical sense.

2. You can take this as a prophecy that will be fulfilled in way that is figurative and spiritual, but absolutely real.

Many Reformed theologians hold this view—a view which says that we believers, who are the temple of the Holy Spirit, will experience the desecrating actions of the Antichrist. We will experience the acute suffering of witnessing the Antichrist's blasphemies and abominations. We—the body of Christ, the temple of the Holy Spirit—will undergo the agony of witnessing this loathsome creature, the Antichrist, exalting himself above God, demanding the worship of the world. We will even experience the unspeakable grief of seeing friends and loved ones bowing down in submission to this satanic monster.

History has seen many antichrists with a small *a*. Various popes and kings and leaders have been suspected of being the biblical Antichrist, especially those who seem murderous, ambitious, and self-glorifying— Napoleon Bonaparte, Hitler, Stalin, Saddam Hussein, and Osama bin Laden, to name a few. It almost seems as though Satan keeps selecting one wicked man after another to practice on until he is finally able to mold and shape his perfect man of sin.

One world leader today who seems to fit the mold of a "small-*a* antichrist" (I'm not suggesting he's the biblical Antichrist) is China's leader Xi Jinping. In the spirit of antichrist, he is establishing himself as the focus of a cult of personality, much as Mao did in the

1950s and 1960s. Xi clearly wants the Chinese people to worship him, not Jesus. Since Xi took power in 2012, the Chinese government has ordered the production of books, music, and dance performances in his honor.[4] In 2017 in Jiangxi province (where Catholic missionary Jean Basset established Christian churches in the seventeenth century), the government told Christians to take down pictures of Jesus and replace them with images of Xi Jinping.[5]

Xi Jinping is also trying to subjugate Chinese Christianity by rewriting the Bible. The new Communist translation of the Bible has not yet been released, but portions have become public. For example, the Communist version of John 8—the story of Jesus and the woman caught in adultery—shows how this outrageous effort to destroy God's Word seems directly inspired by Satan himself.

In the original text, Jesus tells the crowd of accusers, "Let any one of you who is without sin be the first to throw a stone at her." Then He bends down and writes in the dust with His finger. The accusers turn and go, leaving Jesus and the woman alone. Jesus says, "Woman, where are they? Has no one condemned you?" She says, "No one, sir." Jesus says, "Then neither do I condemn you. Go now and leave your life of sin" (John 8:7, 10–11).

Now brace yourself for the Communist version of this story: After the crowd of accusers departs, Jesus tells the woman, "I too am a sinner. But if the law could only be executed by men without blemish, the law would be dead." Then Jesus picks up stones Himself—*and He stones the woman to death.* This is blasphemy on every level. It slanders the sinless character and deity of Jesus, it stands His message of forgiveness on its head, and it falsely makes Jesus an endorser of Communism's brutal, murderous enforcement of its godless laws.[6]

As we approach the climax of human history, we can expect to see an increase in many forms of blasphemy such as this—not only in Communist China but around the world and in the United States. We, the living temple of the Holy Spirit, will witness the desecrating actions of "small-*a* antichrists" again and again—leading ultimately to the biblical Antichrist, who will commit blasphemies and abominations we cannot even imagine now. This will be an agonizing experience for all who truly love the Lord Jesus Christ and long for His return.

The Urgency of Evangelism

In Matthew 24:15 Jesus says, "So when you see standing in the holy place 'the abomination that causes desolation,' spoken of through the prophet Daniel—let the reader understand." The phrase "let the reader understand" is His way of saying that these words are a warning to believers in the last days. Let the generation living through the end-time read these truths and discern the trials that they are enduring.

He follows these words with a series of warnings: When you see "the abomination that causes desolation," flee! Don't stop to pick up any belongings. Escape! Go! And if people tell you the Messiah is here or there, in the wilderness or in a building, don't believe them. When Jesus the Messiah returns, His appearance will be sudden, brilliant, and unmistakable, like lightning flashing in the sky.

Right now, there is time to share the gospel with neighbors and loved ones and strangers on the street. But that window of opportunity is closing—and one day, it will slam shut. There will be warning signs— Jesus calls them labor pains. Those labor pains of history will increase in intensity as the day of His return approaches. But when that moment arrives in a flash, the offer of salvation will be withdrawn.

The Lord's prophecy of His second coming should motivate both believers and nonbelievers alike. For us, the Lord's followers, this prophecy should fill us with a sense of solemn urgency to reach everyone with the good news of Jesus Christ.

If your neighbor's house was on fire, would you run and pound on his door and urge him to escape and save himself? If you discovered the cure for cancer, would you urgently share it with the world? Of course you would. How, then, knowing that the Lord is returning soon, knowing that the day of judgment is swiftly approaching, could you keep that vital information to yourself?

This prophecy should motivate nonbelievers to think soberly about their lives and their eternal fate. The labor pains of history serve as an alarm of looming judgment. These events, combined with the Lord's prophecy, should motivate nonbelievers to repent and receive Jesus as Lord and Savior.

In verses 16 through 28 the Lord speaks of two events at widely separated points in history. Both are times of terror and destruction. One took place in AD 70 when Jerusalem fell to the Romans after a lengthy siege. In verse 16, Jesus says, "then let those who are in Judea flee to the mountains." This warning is addressed to the Jews in Judea during the Roman occupation.

Jesus is saying that no possession is worth enduring the horrors of the Roman siege in AD 70. But I believe Jesus is also making a spiritual application to this prophecy: there is no possession that is worth risking an eternity without Christ. If money or a career or a sinful habit or any other thing is holding you back from following Jesus—*lay it down now* and flee into the arms of Jesus.

The horror of eternal judgment should focus our minds and hearts on eternal salvation. As Jesus said, "What good will it be for someone to gain the whole world, yet forfeit their soul? Or what can anyone give in exchange for their soul?" (Matt. 16:26).

Jewish, Roman, and Christian accounts of the siege of Jerusalem in AD 70 are truly horrifying. Those who had not died of starvation were slaughtered or enslaved when the Romans entered the city. The great temple of Jerusalem was razed to the ground. That is why Jesus warned them, "Let those who are in Judea flee to the mountains." He warned the people of the terrors that would come upon them forty years later. Because of the Romans' vindictive hatred of the Jews, all the people of Judea would be in danger.

The Jewish people have existed for more than four thousand years, ever since God made his covenant with Abraham. Throughout all those centuries, Satan has been savagely obsessed with destroying the nation of Israel. Satan understood the biblical prophecies of the Messiah. Those prophecies go all the way back to Genesis 3, when God told the serpent, "And I will put enmity between you and the woman, and between your offspring and hers; he will crush your head, and you will strike his heel" (v. 15).

Down through history, the offspring of Satan—wicked kings, dictators, and crazed mobs—have committed horrible atrocities against God's chosen people. The Jews have suffered enslavement, exile, pogroms, diasporas, and the Holocaust. Satan, stirring up his evil offspring, has done his best to destroy the lineage of the Messiah—and he even tried to destroy the Messiah Himself. Why is Satan so obsessed with destroying the Jewish people? It's because he knows that the Messiah—Jesus of Nazareth, the son of David, born of a Jewish virgin—is the centerpiece of God's redemptive plan for humanity.

Again and again, down through history, Satan has tried to thwart God's plan. But on the morning of the first Easter, when Jesus stepped forth from the tomb in resurrection power, Satan's head was crushed. Even so, Satan continues his attacks on the followers of Jesus—and on the people of Israel, the Jews. I have no doubt that it was Satan himself who stirred up the Romans to brutally break through the walls of Jerusalem, slaughtering and enslaving the people, and destroying the temple.

CHAOS AND CONFUSION

The second event Jesus speaks of is signaled in Matthew 24:21 with a small but significant Greek word, *gar*. It's a conjunction that strongly signals conclusion and a transition to a new thought. I believe the NIV translation of this word is weak: "For then [Greek: *gar tote*] there will be great distress, unequaled from the beginning of the world until now—and never to be equaled again."

I believe that when Jesus says "*gar tote*," that phrase should stand out to us like a flashing light. Jesus is making a dramatic transition. He is not merely saying, "For then..." He is saying, "But on that day..." He is making a dramatic shift in perspective, changing His focus from AD 70 to a far future time, just before His return to earth. He is switching from "in those days" to "on that day," the day when history draws to a close.

Immediately before His return, there will be time

of tribulation such as has never occurred before—and never will again. In Revelation 6 to 16, which parallels Jesus' Olivet prophecy, you see the seven seals and seven trumpets and seven bowls of God's wrath—and you find that there is a steady escalation of judgment.

In Matthew 24:22 Jesus says, "If those days had not been cut short, no one would survive, but for the sake of the elect those days will be shortened." The parallel to this passage is Revelation 6:12–13, where John writes, "I watched as he opened the sixth seal. There was a great earthquake. The sun turned black like sackcloth made of goat hair, the whole moon turned blood red, and the stars in the sky fell to earth, as figs drop from a fig tree when shaken by a strong wind." A great earthquake causes the sky to darken—perhaps because of smoke and dust. As a result, the day is shortened and nightfall comes early, allowing God's fleeing followers to escape under the cover of darkness.

Then comes this amazing prediction by the Lord Jesus—a prediction of utter confusion. People will say, "Look, here is the Messiah!" or, "'There he is!" and false messiahs and false prophets will perform deceptive signs and wonders. And many people will gather around these lying teachers, because "wherever there is a carcass, there the vultures will gather" (v. 28).

As we look around at the division and confusion in the world today, we can't help but wonder, "How could the world become even more chaotic and confusing than what we see right now?" But Jesus has the answer to this question: As false messiahs and false prophets multiply, so will chaos and confusion. Those who obey Jesus and flee from the false teaching will not be deceived. Those whose minds are baptized by the clarity and truth of the Word of God will not fall for the lies of the Antichrist. They will not bow down to the false messiah—and they will rescue those around them who are tempted to yield to the Antichrist.

Those who take refuge in the one true Christ, who cling for dear life to biblical truth, who have turned their backs on this dying world and all of its false values—they will not be fooled by false messiahs and false miracle workers. They will be victorious over the chaos and confusion of the end-time.

WEATHERING THE STORM

The most sobering and troubling statement in the Olivet Discourse is in verse 24, where Jesus says, "For false messiahs and false prophets will appear and perform great signs and wonders to deceive, if possible, even the elect." This statement cries out for explanation.

What does Jesus mean, "to deceive, *if possible*, even the elect?" Would it be possible for Satan to deceive genuine Christians into following and worshipping the Antichrist? No. Satan cannot deceive true Christian believers. He can tempt us to sin. He can tempt us to discouragement. He can tempt us to fear. And sometimes we yield to these temptations. But Satan could never deceive us into switching sides and worshipping the Antichrist if we are genuine followers of Christ.

Jesus said in John 10:27–28, "My sheep listen to my voice; I know them, and they follow me. I give them eternal life, and they shall never perish; no one will snatch them out of my hand." Here, Jesus assures us of the eternal security of the believer.

Once a person comes to Christ in full, sincere surrender, no one—not even Satan himself—could ever snatch that person out of the Lord's hand. From cover to cover, the Scriptures make this principle very clear. Genuine believers will not be deceived or destroyed on the day of judgment because our Lord sovereignly protects them.

In Matthew 24:29 Jesus says that the sun and moon will be darkened, the stars will fall, and the heavenly bodies will be shaken. All this will take place as the earth is shaking and millions are dying from disease and starvation. And in the midst of this chaos, false messiahs will continue to deceive the masses.

Undoubtedly, many believers who undergo the pressures and terrors of that day will experience anxiety and their confidence may be shaken. They may experience discouragement and fear—*but their faith will weather the storm.* They will not be deceived. Their salvation will not be lost. Their trust in God will not be destroyed.

How can you prepare now for this uncertain and threatening future? I would urge you to get involved in a small-group Bible study through your local church. Join together with up to a dozen committed believers who will pray with you, study God's Word with you, support you in your struggles, and hold you accountable. Share meals with your group. Go on retreats with them and bond with them. Belonging to a Christ-centered loving community is not a luxury or an option; it's a *necessity* in the Christian life. It will be the key to standing strong and immovable during times of chaos and upheaval.

In verse 25 Jesus says, "See, I have told you ahead of time." In other words, "I have given you plenty of warning. Make sure you are ready and prepared. Don't let that day take you by surprise. Make sure you and your family are ready for the end-time."

Jesus says in verse 27, "For as lightning that comes from the east is visible even in the west, so will be the coming of the Son of Man." Here, Jesus says that His return will not be stretched out over days or weeks. His return will be sudden, startlingly glorious, and visible to the entire world. In Acts 1:9–11 the disciples watched in amazed wonder as Jesus ascended into heaven. As they watched, two angels told them that Jesus would return in the same way they saw Him depart. And John, in Revelation, wrote:

> "Look, he is coming with the clouds," and "every eye will see him, even those who pierced him";

and all peoples on earth "will mourn because of him." So shall it be! Amen.

—REVELATION 1:7

In the Bible, clouds are frequently used as a symbol to represent people. When Jesus returns to earth "with the clouds," it means He is returning with all who have gone before us, and they will be coming with Him to meet us in the air. And every eye will see Him, even those who pierced Him. Elsewhere in Revelation, John writes about the fate of the great and mighty people who have trusted in their worldly power and wealth:

> Then the kings of the earth, the princes, the generals, the rich, the mighty, and everyone else, both slave and free, hid in caves and among the rocks of the mountains. They called to the mountains and the rocks, "Fall on us and hide us from the face of him who sits on the throne and from the wrath of the Lamb!"
>
> —REVELATION 6:15–16

On that day, the most powerful and famous people on earth try to hide from His sight. They will call to the mountains and rocks, "Fall on us!" But there will be no place to hide.

In Matthew 24:28 Jesus uses an odd-sounding expression that was actually a common idiom in Jewish culture of that time. In fact, many people use this same idiom today: "Wherever there is a carcass, there the vultures will gather." What does Jesus mean?

Let's look at the context. Jesus first says that if anyone says, "The Messiah is here" or "The Messiah is there," don't be fooled, don't believe it. If you see a crowd gathering here or there, don't be fooled—you won't find the second coming of Christ out in the wilderness or in a room somewhere. Vultures only gather around a dead carcass. Crowds only gather around false prophets, not the living Messiah.

The return of the living Lord will be much more sudden and spectacular than you can possibly imagine—like a bolt of lightning illuminating the sky from horizon to horizon.

How Should We Respond?

We must ask ourselves, "How should I respond to this message from Jesus, the Lord of history?" I would urge you to take these two actions:

First, *be alert to the "birth pains" of history.* Talk to your friends and family about this message of Jesus from Matthew 24. When events in the news align with the events Jesus predicts as the beginning of labor pains that foreshadow His return, point them out to the people around you. Urge your family and friends to be constantly, spiritually ready for the Lord's return.

Second, *pray for revival.* The late Christian leader Stephen Olford, whom Billy Graham called "the man who most influenced my ministry," has called revival "an invasion from heaven that brings a conscious awareness of God."[7] Do you and I really want to experience that holy invasion of our lives by God's Spirit? Do we want that holy invasion more than we want wealth, success, status, or our secret sins? When we truly desire God more than any other treasure in our lives, and we pray earnestly for revival, then God can bring about a radical transformation in our lives—and the lives of people around us.

You and I live in the here and now, the time God has allotted to us in which we can serve Him faithfully every waking moment. Yet we also have one foot in the world to come, in eternity. As we live and serve in the "here and now," we need to keep our hearts focused on the "yet to come." We need to live each moment as if Jesus were returning in mere seconds.

His coming will be sudden and unexpected—but those who are prepared for His return will not be caught by surprise. They will not be dismayed. They will be full of joy when, like a flash of lightning, Jesus returns to take us home.

Chapter 4

THE FINAL SIGN

N 1841 POET Robert Browning wrote: "God's in his heaven—All's right with the world!"—from *Pippa Passes*, Act I: Morning.[1] Yes, God is in heaven and He's in ultimate control of history. Nothing that happens catches Him by surprise. But as for the statement, "All's right with the world"—nothing could be further from the truth.

Like a flood of water being held back behind a massive dam, the great day of the Lord's return is being held back until the appointed day. There are growing signs that His return may be growing near. In churches and home Bible studies, on social media, and in casual discussions, Christians ask: What do today's global events mean? If God is on the throne, why does the world seem completely out of control?

America, once considered a Christian nation, is now clearly a *post*-Christian nation—and is well on its way to becoming an *anti*-Christian nation. As we see the persecution of Christians increasing worldwide and even in America, we must ask ourselves, "Are we approaching the end-time? Is the Lord Jesus returning soon?"

SIGNS IN THE HEAVENS

In the Olivet Discourse, Jesus has been telling the disciples about a time we call the great tribulation. Next, beginning with Matthew 24:29, He tells them what happens *after* the great tribulation:

> Immediately after the distress of those days "the sun will be darkened, and the moon will not give its light; the stars will fall from the sky, and the heavenly bodies will be shaken."
>
> Then will appear the sign of the Son of Man in heaven. And then all the peoples of the earth will mourn when they see the Son of Man coming on the clouds of heaven, with power and great glory. And he will send his angels with a loud trumpet call, and they will gather his elect from the four winds, from one end of the heavens to the other.
>
> Now learn this lesson from the fig tree: As soon as its twigs get tender and its leaves come out, you know that summer is near. Even so,

when you see all these things, you know that it is near, right at the door. Truly I tell you, this generation will certainly not pass away until all these things have happened. Heaven and earth will pass away, but my words will never pass away.

—MATTHEW 24:29–35

Throughout the history of the church, faithful followers of the Lord Jesus Christ have looked forward eagerly to our Lord's return. The second coming of Christ has been a powerful motivation for Christians to live righteously and share the good news, generation after generation.

The whole world celebrates the *first* advent of Jesus—the event we call Christmas. Even nonbelievers celebrate Christmas. But as I survey the Christian landscape, it seems that only a tiny remnant of believers truly looks forward to His *second* coming. My prayer for the church is that many Christians will experience the excitement and expectation of eagerly awaiting the Lord's return.

In verses 29–31 our Lord describes the supreme signs that immediately precede His coming: The sun will be darkened. The moon will not give its light. The stars will fall from the sky. The powers of the heavens will be shaken.

A few years ago the signs Jesus describes would seem scientifically unthinkable. In recent years, however, scientists have begun to worry about exactly the kind of catastrophe Jesus describes.

Did you know that NASA has a Planetary Defense Coordination Office? Its mission is to protect planet Earth from bombardment by asteroids.

On November 23, 2021, NASA's Planetary Defense team launched a spacecraft from Vandenberg Space Force Base in California. The spacecraft is programmed to smash into an asteroid at fifteen thousand miles per hour and change the asteroid's orbit. Impact will take place in the fall of 2022. If the test is successful, NASA expects to be able to deflect any Earth-threatening asteroid and avoid a global catastrophe.[2]

There are many so-called "near-Earth asteroids"—asteroids that circle the sun in an orbit that comes very close to Earth's orbit. One asteroid that makes scientists lose sleep at night is 99942 Apophis, which is about as long as four football fields. In 2029 Apophis (named for the Egyptian god of destruction) will pass about twenty thousand miles from Earth's surface and will be visible to the naked eye. (For comparison, the moon is about two hundred fifty thousand miles away.) Scientists are tracking dozens of near-Earth asteroids, many of them large enough to destroy a city or endanger civilization.[3]

I thank God for science, the discipline of discovering everything God has set in motion in the universe. My faith, however, is not in science, but in the God who created the universe and made science possible. Jesus said that before His return the universe will begin to disintegrate, rapidly and catastrophically.

One of the effects of that disintegration is that the solar system will be thrown into chaos, along with the rest of the universe. Objects like 99942 Apophis will no longer be traveling in mathematically predictable orbits, but will career wildly. Some will likely rain upon the Earth, like stars falling from the sky, exploding, destroying cities, triggering massive earthquakes and tidal waves.

In the parallel account in Luke, Jesus says:

> There will be signs in the sun, moon and stars. On the earth, nations will be in anguish and perplexity at the roaring and tossing of the sea. People will faint from terror, apprehensive of what is coming on the world, for the heavenly bodies will be shaken.
>
> —LUKE 21:25–26

To "faint from terror," in Scripture, is to die of fright. In the original language, the phrase "will faint from terror" is a single Greek word, *apopsychō*, which means "to breathe out life, to expire." Jesus is saying that strong men will literally stop breathing because of their terror.

At the coming of Jesus Christ, the powers of heaven and earth will be shaken. There will not be a place of safety anywhere on the earth. Nations and populations will be in panic as the universe seems to come apart at the seams.

Hebrews 1:3 tells us that Jesus the Son is "the radiance of God's glory," and that He is continually "sustaining all things by his powerful word." He upholds everything from the electrons whirling around the nuclei of atoms to the stars wheeling in vast galaxies.

But on that day, Jesus will withhold His sustaining power. All it will take is for Him to suspend that universe-making power for a nanosecond—and instantly, stars and galaxies will fly apart. Why? Because all stable reference points of the natural order will be suspended. All the laws of nature will be repealed.

On planet Earth, which is held together by the will and power of God, the suspension of the laws of nature for even a nanosecond would produce thousands of tsunamis and earthquakes—all at once. Seven hundred years before Christ the prophet Isaiah prophesied of that day:

> The stars of heaven and their constellations will not show their light. The rising sun will be darkened and the moon will not give its light.
>
> —ISAIAH 13:10

The Bible is nothing if not consistent.

When will Jesus appear? Immediately after these events take place. This cosmic cataclysm will affect every part of the globe, every nation on earth, every human being on the planet. All eyes will observe these signs. And as everyone is watching the skies, the Son of God will appear.

THE FINAL SIGN

Matthew 24:30 tells us that the appearance of Jesus will be the final sign: "Then will appear the sign of the Son of Man in heaven. And then all the peoples of the earth will mourn when they see the Son of Man coming on the clouds of heaven, with power and great glory."

As the entire human race is reeling from these catastrophes, the Lord Jesus Christ will be manifested in all of His splendor, glory, and righteousness. In the darkness of midnight, He will shine like the noonday sun. In the midst of devastation and tribulation, the Prince of Peace will appear—and everyone on Earth will mourn.

Those who have rejected Him will try to hide from Him, but there will be nowhere to hide. Those who have scorned His name and have persecuted His followers will be ashamed. Those who have blasphemed Him and have tried to erase His name from public life will writhe in an agony of regret.

Among those who will be ashamed are those who call themselves Christians but have brought error and falsehood into the church. They call their movement the "emerging church" or "progressive Christianity" or "post-evangelical Christianity." They deny the existence of heaven and hell. They deny the final judgment. They deny the atonement for sin Jesus paid on the cross. They deny the resurrection. They deny the second coming of Christ. They adhere to a form of the Christian faith while denying its power—and in so doing, they have led many people, including many young people, into soul-destroying deception and error.

At the dark climax of history's midnight, at the apex of the cosmic calamity, after the human race has passed through economic, social, political, and spiritual catastrophe on an unprecedented scale—Jesus will manifest Himself in infinite majesty and glory.

Can you imagine what that moment will be like? Can you imagine the sight of the Lord Jesus appearing in blazing glory?

All who have rebelled against Him, cursed Him, rejected Him, blasphemed Him, and tormented His followers will mourn their sins—and they'll have no hope of redemption. All who have twisted God's Word, killed and oppressed God's followers, and burned Christian churches will weep for what they have done—and they'll have no hope of forgiveness.

Celebrities and superstars who were once worshipped by adoring fans will seek anonymity among the rocks and invisibility in the caves. Kings, dictators, and leaders will try to flee from Him who sits on the throne.

We must take special notice of the last five words in verse 30: "with power and great glory." Jesus will arrive on the clouds of heaven, *with power and great glory.* His power has already been demonstrated by these cataclysmic events that have shaken the heavens. But as awesome and terrifying as these events have been, they hardly compare to what these events mean to us as believers.

On that day, He will demonstrate His power by overthrowing Satan and the demonic forces once and for all. He will demonstrate His power in saving and protecting His elect. He will demonstrate His power by establishing His rule in righteousness.

On that day, He will demonstrate His power by conquering His enemies. He will demonstrate His power by destroying the Antichrist. He will demonstrate His power by destroying those who worship the beast. He will demonstrate His power by destroying the power of sin.

On that day, He will demonstrate His power by bringing everlasting righteousness and peace to all who put their trust in Him. He will demonstrate His power by ending the threat of droughts, floods, tornadoes, earthquakes, famine, and plagues. His power will wipe away all tears. His power will end diseases from cancer to Alzheimer's to Parkinson's to COVID. He will demonstrate His power by eliminating hatred, prejudice, racism, murder, injustice, lies, and the lust for one person to control or enslave another.

In the Book of Acts, when the resurrected Lord Jesus ascended into heaven, two angels, dressed in white, promised the disciples that Jesus would return: "'Men of Galilee,' they said, 'why do you stand here looking into the sky? This same Jesus, who has been taken from you into heaven, will come back in the same way you have seen him go into heaven'" (Acts 1:11). When Jesus returns with power and great glory, the angels' promise to the disciples will be fulfilled.

How will the power and great glory of Jesus be manifested? In the shaking of the heavens. In the downfall and destruction of Satan and his demons. In the salvation of the elect. In the restoration of the new heaven and the new earth. In Jesus' visible reign over the new creation. In the final elimination of sin and death.

THE PARABLE OF THE FIG TREE

The arrival of Jesus will bring about a beautiful and lasting era of peace and innocence—just as the prophet Isaiah foretold:

> The wolf will live with the lamb, the leopard will
> lie down with the goat, the calf and the lion and
> the yearling together; and a little child will lead
> them.
>
> —ISAIAH 11:6

That is the new reality Jesus will usher in when He comes with power and great glory. He will take His place on His glorious throne—*and we shall see Him as He is.*

No human being has ever seen God as He is. Adam and Eve only saw a glimpse of God's glory when they walked in the cool of the day with Him. The children of Israel saw only a glimpse of His glory as the mighty pillars of fire and cloud went before them in the wilderness. Peter, James, and John stood on the Mount of Transfiguration and they saw Jesus' face shine like the sun and His garment glowing white—but that was only a glimpse of His glory.

One day you and I will see the full and unimpeded glory of God in Jesus Christ—and the sight will leave us overwhelmed in awe, completely speechless.

In Matthew 24:31 Jesus tells us, "And he will send his angels with a loud trumpet call, and they will gather his elect from the four winds, from one end of the heavens to the other." The sound of the trumpet always signals a major announcement. Here, the angels issue a trumpet call assembling God's elect from every corner of the planet.

Next, Jesus tells His disciples a parable—the Parable of the Fig Tree (vv. 32–33). He tells them, "Now learn this lesson from the fig tree: As soon as its twigs get tender and its leaves come out, you know that summer is near. Even so, when you see all these things, you know that it is near, right at the door."

Many people enjoy finding an allegory in all of Jesus' parables. They frequently interpret this parable to mean that the fig tree represents the political state of Israel. I am as strong a supporter of the modern state of Israel as anyone, but I don't believe the Lord Jesus is using the fig tree to represent Israel.

Our Lord is not telling the disciples to look forward to 1948 and the establishment of the state of Israel. The disciples would not have been able to understand the parable if that's what it meant.

Others say that the budding leaves of the fig tree represent a spiritual revival in Israel. But modern Israel, as you know, is a very secular nation. I had the privilege of preaching in several Messianic synagogues in Israel. I have many Messianic Jewish friends in Israel. There are strong Jewish Christian believers in Israel—but I don't believe this parable refers to a national revival in Israel.

In fact, I believe the Parable of the Fig Tree is far less complicated than many people make it to be. Jesus is giving the disciples a parable to make it easy for them— and subsequent generations—to understand the signs of His return.

In the time of Jesus, Palestine was filled with fig trees. Almost every Jewish backyard had a fig tree, so the people were familiar with these trees and their ways. The fig tree is often used in the Bible to illustrate one thing, just as Jesus uses it here. He is saying that, when the branches become tender and put forth its leaves, it is springtime. And when it is springtime, summer isn't far behind.

When new leaves bud on the branches, put away your sweater. Even children knew that. Spring means that the harvest of the delicious fruit is around the corner. Throughout the Gospel of Matthew, the harvest symbolizes judgment. It's the time when the wheat is separated from the chaff—when believers are separated from nonbelievers. When the wheat is harvested and goes into the barn, the chaff is to be burned.

Our Lord is saying that when you see the fig leaves, you know the time of harvest is coming. And when you see the signs that Jesus speaks of, the day of judgment is around the corner. He is speaking not only to the disciples, but to all believers who are living immediately before His return. He is saying, "Wake up before it's too late. Learn from the fig tree. It is springtime now—but the summer of harvest and judgment is not far off."

Friend in Christ, I believe with all my heart that this separation is about to begin.

What Generation?

In verses 33–34 Jesus makes His meaning plain: "Even so, when you see all these things, you know that it is near, right at the door. Truly I tell you, this generation will certainly not pass away until all these things have happened."

"This generation"? What generation does Jesus refer to? The generation He was speaking to, the disciples? Obviously not.

Yet some critics and atheists have taken His statement that way. They have foolishly said that Jesus was confused, that the Bible is contradictory, that He was predicting His return within the lifetime of the disciples. How can He say that "this generation will certainly not pass away" when the disciples eventually died?

Yet the construction of the sentence makes it clear that He is speaking of the generation that will see the shoots of the fig tree, the generation that will witness the "labor pains" of history, the generation that will witness the tribulations and cosmic catastrophes. This generation will be alive at the return of Christ. This generation will not pass away until *all* these things have happened.

Remember, the Olivet Discourse opens with the disciples in verse 3 asking Jesus, "Tell us...when will this [the destruction of the temple] happen, and what will be the sign of your coming and of the end of the age?" They probably assumed that the destruction of the temple and end of the age would occur at roughly the same time. They didn't understand that these two events might be separated by centuries.

So Jesus answered both questions in one discourse, speaking of "those days" (when the temple would be destroyed in AD 70) and "that day," the end of the age. Speaking of the end of the age, Jesus said that it would occur very soon after these signs are witnessed. The generation that would see the signs would be alive to witness the great and final sign, the return of Jesus with power and great glory.

You and I may well be that generation. Does this thought fill you with fear—or joy unspeakable? If it fills you with fear, then you have not surrendered your life fully to Christ. Those who are completely surrendered to Him are eagerly awaiting His return. If you have never come to the Lord Jesus, confessing your sin, and receiving Him as your Lord and Savior, I urge you to do so now.

Those who will be terrified on that day are the ones who have refused His gracious invitation. Ever since Jesus stretched out His arms on the cross, those arms have been wide open to welcome anyone who comes to Him for forgiveness and eternal life. We are all sinners—but sinners who have received His grace are longing to see His return. Only the sinners who have rejected His grace fear His return.

If you have never surrendered your life to Jesus Christ, please do so now. Before you turn the page, I encourage you to pray this prayer in all sincerity:

> *Dear Lord Jesus, I have sinned against You. I'm so sorry for my sin. I repent and ask You to forgive me. I know that You love me and that You died on the cross to save me. Have mercy on me, Lord, and blot out my sin. Make my heart clean. Fill me with Your Holy Spirit. Help me to live every day to please You. Thank You, Lord, for saving me so that I will spend eternity with You. Amen.*

CHANGE BEGINS WITH US

In verse 35, Jesus makes this astonishing statement: "Heaven and earth will pass away, but my words will never pass away." Clearly, He does not want anyone to take this message lightly. The words of the Olivet Discourse will outlast the entire universe.

The galaxies will collapse on themselves. The stars will grow cold. The earth may die in a hailstorm of exploding asteroids. But every word Jesus prophesied will be fulfilled.

Nobody knows the day or the hour of that fulfilment. That is why we need to pray for revival in our lives, our families, our churches, our nation, and our world.

It is obvious to every genuine believer that America is going through morally dark days. I often hear Christians speak despairingly of the times in which we live. Moral degeneracy is so pervasive in our entertainment media, our social media, and across the internet that it's easy to believe that revival is impossible, that our moral and spiritual collapse is inevitable.

Many people once thought of America as a Christian nation, always morally strong—until recently, when the nation began a steep downhill slide. In fact, this is not the first time America has fallen into a moral and spiritual abyss. America fell into moral bankruptcy soon after the Revolutionary War.

J. Edwin Orr (1912–1987) was a minister and an evangelist for Campus Crusade for Christ. Dr. Billy Graham called him "one of the greatest authorities on the history of religious revivals in the Protestant world."[4] Orr chronicled the moral collapse that occurred after the Revolution: "Drunkenness became epidemic. Out of a population of five million, 300,000 were confirmed drunkards; Profanity was of the most shocking kind.... Women were afraid to go out at night for fear of assault. Bank robberies were a daily occurrence."[5]

Churches at that time were in a terrible state. Methodist, Baptist, Presbyterian, and Congregationalist churches were all dwindling in membership. The Lutherans and Episcopalians had lost so many members that they considered merging, despite their theological differences.

Orr observed that some of the leaders of the Revolution became pessimists about the future of Christianity in America. The Chief Justice of the Supreme Court, John Marshall, wrote to James Madison, the father of the Constitution, that the Christian church "was too far gone ever to be redeemed." And Thomas Paine, one of the intellectual leaders of the Revolution, said, "Christianity will be forgotten in thirty years."[6]

Then as now, the colleges and universities became breeding grounds for atheists, agnostics, and enemies of Christianity. Orr writes that a poll of the Harvard student body found not a single Christian believer on the campus. A similar poll taken at Princeton found only two believers. Only five Princeton students did not belong to the so-called "filthy speech movement," which promoted profanity and obscenity on campus. Students at other schools rioted, held mock communions, and burned a Bible at a public bonfire.

"Christians were so few on campus in the 1790s," Orr concludes, "that they met in secret, like a communist cell, and kept their minutes in code so that no one would know."[7]

In 1794, when America's moral state was at its worst, a pastor named Isaac Backus sent letters to pastors of every Christian denomination across New England. He urged those pastors to set up a network of prayer meetings on the first Monday of each month. At the meetings, which Backus called "a concert of prayer," believers were to pray earnestly for revival in America.

Backus had been influenced by the Great Awakening that swept England and the thirteen American colonies in the 1730s and 1740s. The prayer movement Backus founded quickly snowballed into the Second Great Awakening, which lasted from the 1790s into the 1840s. Out of the Second Great Awakening came the modern missionary movement, the abolition movement, Sunday schools, evangelistic campaigns, and all the benefits that come from a moral and righteous society.[8]

Friend in Christ, change can and will happen when God's people repent of their sin and turn to Him. Revival starts with repentance, and repentance starts with you and me.

It does no good to complain about the state of

the world, the state of the government, or the state of society. Change must begin with us. When God's people repent of their sin and turn to Him and become fervent in prayer—then watch out!

God is going to move among His people.

Chapter 5

THE NOAH IMPERATIVE

I MUST BEGIN THIS chapter with a solemn warning.

If you are a parent or grandparent of school-age children, I need to warn you that this chapter contains information that you will find shocking and disturbing. There are people in positions of power and influence who have targeted the souls of your children or grandchildren for destruction. I will detail this plot against the children later in this chapter, but I didn't want to drop this information on you without a word of caution.

In this next section of the Olivet Discourse, Jesus says, "As it was in the days of Noah, so it will be at the coming of the Son of Man" (Matt. 24:37). What were the days of Noah like? Genesis 6:5 tells us, "The LORD saw how great the wickedness of the human race had become on the earth, and that every inclination of the thoughts of the human heart was only evil all the time."

As we watch the news and see the wickedness all around us, we can't help but conclude that the days we live in have much in common with the days of Noah. We see widespread corruption and dishonesty in our government, greed and disloyalty in our corporations, and lust and blasphemy in our media. I can think of few more wicked acts than to seek to destroy the innocence of children, as many in our education establishment are now doing.

Jesus solemnly warned us in Matthew 18:6. "If anyone causes one of these little ones—those who believe in me—to stumble, it would be better for them to have a large millstone hung around their neck and to be drowned in the depths of the sea." In this twenty-first-century version of the days of Noah, we would need thousands and thousands of millstones to deal with the evil now being committed against our children—as you will soon see.

SCOFFERS AND WORRIERS

Whenever the subject of the Lord's return is discussed, people seem to fall into two camps: (1) those who try to predict the date of His return and (2) those who are skeptical and apathetic about the Lord's return. Jesus tells us that His genuine followers will watch for His return. In Matthew 24:36–39, Jesus shows us how we should live out our lives as we eagerly anticipate His return.

If you carefully study and heed the Scriptures, there can be little doubt that the return of the Lord is imminent. Though only the Father knows the exact hour of Christ's return, Jesus Himself said in Matthew 24:44, "So you also must be ready, because the Son of Man will come at an hour when you do not expect him." And the apostle Peter tells us:

> Above all, you must understand that in the last days scoffers will come, scoffing and following their own evil desires. They will say, "Where is this 'coming' he promised? Ever since our ancestors died, everything goes on as it has since the beginning of creation."
>
> —2 PETER 3:3–4

The irony is that we live in a time when scoffers are in a state of panic over the signs of approaching catastrophe. They fear the wrath of Mother Earth because of climate change. They fear the wrath of the Almighty Dollar because of looming economic collapse. They fear the wrath of the God of War as Communist China plunges the world into a new nuclear arms race. They even fear the wrath of the skies, worrying that an asteroid might hurtle to earth and wipe out all life on the planet.

They fear that the end of the world may be upon us—but they do not fear God's wrath. They scoff at the

Lord's promise to return with power and great glory. Following their own evil desires, they say, "Where is this 'second coming of Christ' you Christians believe in? It's been two thousand years, and the world keeps spinning, people keep sinning—and I don't see any sign that Jesus is returning anytime soon."

While scientists worry that civilization may perish due to climate change or nuclear war or a random asteroid collision, those of us who love the Lord Jesus and trust the Word of God have no fear of that day. We believe in being good stewards of the earth God has made, and we believe in being peacemakers and trying to avert war. We trust that God is in control of the future, and we can face the future without fear. In fact, we *eagerly* look forward to the Lord's return.

We are not like those doomsday cultists of the past who sold all their belongings, put on white robes, climbed to the mountaintops, and waited for the mothership to descend from space and take them away. As followers of Christ, as servants of the Lord, we work hard, we serve faithfully, we give generously, we share the good news enthusiastically, we love one another devotedly, we forgive each other readily, and that is how we await the Lord's return.

We are soldiers engaged in spiritual battle, cheerfully proclaiming the gospel while battling evil. When Jesus returns on that day, may He find us serving Him and rescuing sinners.

"As It Was in the Days of Noah"

Let's hear the next crucial section of the Olivet Discourse, in which the Lord Jesus compares the end-time to a key event in the Book of Genesis:

> But about that day or hour no one knows, not even the angels in heaven, nor the Son, but only the Father. As it was in the days of Noah, so it will be at the coming of the Son of Man. For in the days before the flood, people were eating and drinking, marrying and giving in marriage, up to the day Noah entered the ark; and they knew nothing about what would happen until the flood came and took them all away. That is how it will be at the coming of the Son of Man.
> —MATTHEW 24:36–39

Here we see one of the clearest signs that the return of the Lord is imminent: "As it was in the days of Noah, so it will be at the coming of the Son of Man." In other words, the same godless attitudes, hatreds, lusts, bloodthirstiness, and moral depravity that character-ized Noah's time will prevail in the end-time. Let's go back to Genesis 6 and recall exactly what the days of Noah were like. Genesis 6:1 tells us that in Noah's time "human beings began to increase in number on the earth." Then a few verses down we read:

> The LORD saw how great the wickedness of the human race had become on the earth, and that

every inclination of the thoughts of the human heart was only evil all the time. The LORD regretted that he had made human beings on the earth, and his heart was deeply troubled. So the LORD said, "I will wipe from the face of the earth the human race I have created—and with them the animals, the birds and the creatures that move along the ground—for I regret that I have made them." But Noah found favor in the eyes of the LORD.

—GENESIS 6:5–8

It is fashionable today for some pastors to cater to the unbelief of worldly churchgoers. They say, "You don't have to believe that the flood of Noah was a real historical event."

Oh, yes, you do! If Jesus, who coexisted with God the Father before the creation of the world, says it happened, then it happened. To disbelieve the story of the flood of Noah is to question the integrity of the Savior. And how can you worship Christ as Savior and Lord if you can't trust His integrity?

Both Old and New Testaments affirm that the flood is a historic event. And the important feature of the flood that Jesus affirms is that it came at a time of great sin and rebellion against God, it came suddenly, and those who rejected the invitation to be saved were taken by surprise.

What were the days of Noah like?

The first characteristic of those days is population

growth: "Human beings began to increase in number on the earth." There is nothing wrong with population growth per se. In fact, Genesis 1:28 tells us that, after God created the human race, He "blessed them and said to them, 'Be fruitful and increase in number; fill the earth and subdue it.'"

But an increase of population often brings with it an increase of moral decadence and sin. In 1972 there were roughly half as many people in the world—about 3.8 billion. By 2022 the world's population neared 7.9 billion people. In 50 years, from 1972 to 2022, the population of the world more than doubled.

At the time of Christ the world population stood at about 200 million. By AD 1200 the world population had doubled to about 400 million. By the time of the American Revolution, in 1776, the world population had doubled again, to about 800 million. The population doubled again by 1900, to about 1.6 billion. The population doubled again by 1960, to more than 3 billion.[1] From the time of Christ the population doubles in increasingly short periods of time—first 1,200 years, then less than 600 years, then less than 125 years, then 50 years.

Our ability to produce food has grown along with the population—to a point. In recent years we have seen riots over food shortages in various parts of the world—in West Bengal, India, in 2007, in Venezuela in 2016–2017, and in South Africa in 2021, where rioting escalated into nationwide grocery store looting. In the

United States, fears of shortages during the COVID pandemic resulted in panic-buying and hoarding.

The Book of Revelation tells us that in the end-time, food will become scarce and expensive: "Then I heard what sounded like a voice among the four living creatures, saying, 'Two pounds of wheat for a day's wages, and six pounds of barley for a day's wages, and do not damage the oil and the wine!'" (Rev. 6:6). Even now many of our fellow believers around the world live from hand to mouth.

As the population continues to increase, there is no guarantee that our food production and supply chain will keep pace. According to the Global Network Against Food Crises, more than 155 million people in fifty-five countries suffered acute hunger during 2020, up from 135 million the previous year. The direct causes of these famines include war, extreme weather, economic crises, and the COVID-19 pandemic. Experts from the United States, the European Union, and the United Nations issued a joint statement declaring, "The outlook for 2021 and beyond is grim."[2]

We live in a time like the days of Noah because the world's population is growing at an unsustainable rate. As a result, a humanitarian catastrophe looms on the horizon.

UNPRECEDENTED ACCUMULATION OF KNOWLEDGE

Genesis 4 tells us that the preflood era was a time of unprecedented accumulation of knowledge. Verse 17 speaks of the building of cities, and verse 22 tells us of the beginnings of the science of metallurgy. Though God instructed Noah in how to build the ark, he undoubtedly had to bring a certain level of knowledge of woodworking and construction to the task, suggesting that such knowledge was widespread in the culture of that time. The ark was comparable in size to one of our ocean liners today—450 feet long by 75 feet wide by some calculations—so its construction was quite a feat of engineering.

Our own time resembles the days of Noah in that these too are days of innovation and the rapid increase in knowledge. Before 1900 human knowledge doubled roughly every hundred years. By the end of World War II human knowledge doubled every twenty-five years. Today, experts believe that human knowledge doubles every thirteen months—and an IBM study claims that because of advances in artificial intelligence and the internet, human knowledge will soon be doubling *every twelve hours.*[3]

In general, knowledge is a good thing. But knowledge without godly wisdom can be dangerous. For example, a September 2021 article in the *Atlantic* offers evidence that the COVID-19 pandemic may have originated as a "gain-of-function experiment gone wrong"—a project that took an infectious bat coronavirus into the laboratory and genetically enhanced it to make it more infectious in human beings.[4] Researchers engaging in such a dangerous experiment would undoubtedly have a lot of knowledge. But anyone who would recklessly put the entire planet at risk seems arrogant and unwise beyond belief.

Knowledge without wisdom produces egotism, greed, selfishness, pride, and wickedness. That is exactly the social and spiritual context of Noah's day. As Genesis tells us, "The LORD saw how great the wickedness of the human race had become on the earth, and that every inclination of the thoughts of the human heart was only evil all the time."

It was human wickedness that brought the judgment of God upon the human race. And if human wickedness in Noah's day was so awful that God had to drown humanity with a flood, imagine the stench of wickedness that our own wicked society gives off. Today, in our media, on our social media, on our campuses, everywhere we turn, human beings not only ignore God but mock and revile God. Humanity overwhelmingly treats God's moral absolutes with contempt.

Everywhere, violence and theft are on the rise. Government, which God established to maintain order, protect the innocent, and punish the guilty, now indulges and even encourages rioting, looting, arson, and mass violence. For five months in 2020, American cities were burned and looted while mayors ordered police to stand down and permit the mayhem to go on.

In October 2021 the Walgreens drugstore chain announced the closure of many stores in San Francisco because city officials refused to prosecute shoplifting and other crimes. City officials have essentially legalized crime, turning San Francisco into a haven of lawlessness.[5]

SHEDDING OF INNOCENT BLOOD

One of the worst forms of human wickedness imaginable is genocide—the deliberate, systematic annihilation (in whole or in part) of a racial, ethnic, or religious group. After the Holocaust perpetrated by Nazi Germany against the Jews, the nations of the world vowed, "Never again!" Despite that vow, genocide has continued on into the twenty-first century.

The first genocide of the twenty-first century was in the Darfur region in western Sudan. Ethnically Arab militias began massacring non-Arab people in 2003, and the killings are still going on today.

In the Rakhine state of northwestern Myanmar/Burma, the officially Buddhist government engages in systematic persecution of the Muslim Rohingya people.

When the so-called Islamic State or ISIS conquered large parts of Syria and Iraq in 2014–2015, the terror group began to systematically slaughter Yazidis, Shiites, and Assyrian Christians. ISIS tactics include mass murder, rape, and the destruction of entire villages.

In South Sudan, which has been torn by ethnic civil war since 2013, ethnic violence and mass slaughter are daily occurrences.

And when it comes to Communist China, the world

continues to do business with a regime that engages in political oppression, slavery, and genocide.

But we don't have to go abroad to find mass slaughter on a horrifying scale—and people who rationalize it. Today, even many self-described "Christians" make excuses for the abortion industry, minimizing the shedding of innocent blood across America.

Wickedness is on the increase worldwide. The internet festers with it. Many churches today deemphasize the awfulness of sin and ignore biblical morality. Sexual immorality among Christians is rampant. Many Christians no longer view homosexual behavior as an affront to God and a rebellion against His creation, but as a valid lifestyle choice. In recent years, a number of prominent evangelical pastors have turned out to be drug addicts, alcoholics, and even sexual predators. And if the shepherds have lost their way, what hope is there for the flock?

Today, increasing numbers of churchgoers no longer believe in biblical morality, in the virgin birth, in the resurrection of Jesus, in the coming judgment, or that Satan is a real being. The hearts of many in the church have become hardened. As the apostle Paul wrote, "For the time will come when people will not put up with sound doctrine. Instead, to suit their own desires, they will gather around them a great number of teachers to say what their itching ears want to hear" (2 Tim. 4:3). Clearly, the time that Paul foresaw is now upon us.

Many in the church are running from preacher to

preacher, looking for a sermon that will tell them what they want to hear, not what the Word of God says. And they have plenty of apostate churches and preachers to choose from.

THE DESTRUCTION OF INNOCENT YOUNG SOULS

As I stated at the beginning of this chapter, I'm about to give you some of the worst news I have ever written in a book: the souls of your children and grandchildren have been targeted for destruction by Marxists—not Marxists in China or some other Communist nation. These Marxists are in your government-run American public school system. They are determined to rob your children and grandchildren of their innocence.

You might be surprised to learn that Marxism is rampant in our educational system—and to be clear, I'm not suggesting that your child's teacher is necessarily a Marxist. But, unfortunately, the teachers don't always have very much control over what the education establishment requires them to teach.

In America today, all the commanding heights of the culture are controlled by a secular Left mindset known under such labels as Cultural Marxism, Neo-Marxism, Western Marxism, Progressivism, and Wokeism. It is an ideology that views Western culture in general (and Judeo-Christian culture in particular) as the primary source of human oppression. Leftists control the universities, the entertainment media, the news and information media, social media, and many major corporations.

Mathematician and culture critic James Lindsay is probably the world's leading authority on this radical Left movement. With Helen Pluckrose, Lindsay coauthored the 2020 book *Cynical Theories: How Activist Scholarship Made Everything About Race, Gender, and Identity—and Why This Harms Everybody*. In a November 2021 podcast, Lindsay warns that the neo-Marxist woke agenda is targeting our kids for sexual and gender-identity indoctrination.

"One of the targets that woke culture wants to dismantle," Lindsay says, "is the innocence of children.... These critical theories...see the innocence of children as a fundamental problem that has to be overcome in order to achieve [the children's] 'liberation.' They seek to achieve the sexual liberation of children, to achieve gender liberation, to achieve racial liberation."[6]

Lindsay cites the example of the Genderbread Person, a cartoon image used to indoctrinate schoolchildren into today's woke theory of gender (you can see the Genderbread Person for yourself at www.genderbread.org). Superimposed on an image we traditionally call a "gingerbread man," there is a brain labeled "identity," a heart labeled "attraction," an outline labeled "expression" (meaning, the expression of sexual feelings), and a symbol labeled "sex" where the private parts would be. The purpose of the Genderbread Person is to create confusion in the child's mind about whether his or her "identity," "attraction," and "sexual expression" matches his or her biological sex.

Lindsay says that even elementary schools have become indoctrination centers for "gender theory and neo-Marxist queer theory" along with "the racialization of children in schools," all of which is designed to "obliterate the innocence of children." In fact, if you were to visit your child's school library, Lindsay says, there's a good chance you'd find shockingly explicit books depicting sexual activity involving schoolchildren.[7]

One Fairfax, Virginia, mom visited her kids' school library and checked out books that she held up and described at a September 2021 school board meeting. "Both of these books include pedophilia," she told the board. "Sex between men and boys." I will spare you the graphic details she described as she held up the books— but the fact that our schoolchildren could obtain such explicit pornography from the school library should shock and anger every parent and grandparent.

As this mother spoke, school board members interrupted and tried to silence her, saying, "There are children in the audience here!"—apparently oblivious to the irony that there are also schoolchildren in the library where she checked out the obscene books.[8]

THE ABOLITION OF THE FAMILY

Why are public schools exposing schoolchildren to pornography? James Lindsay says the education establishment has a deliberate strategy to "break down childhood innocence...literally to destabilize individuals as children and to make them susceptible to politically actionable points of view....If they can't understand themselves...then they're very easily politically manipulable, they will be depressed, they will be anxious, they will be groomable....This destabilization [of children] is quite intentional."

In other words, Marxist strategists in the education establishment know that children who question their own sexual identity can be politically "groomed" to become leftists because the radical Left welcomes and celebrates every form of sexual aberration. A psychologically stable and confident child cannot be easily swayed. That's why Marxists want to take stable children from stable homes and destabilize them, psychologically and sexually.

"This is a long-running project, rooted in Marxist theory," says Lindsay, "that's being used specifically to destabilize the relationship between parents and children, childhood and adulthood, very intentionally.... The Marxists know what they're doing." They are destabilizing children so they can "manipulate [them] into being revolutionaries for their cause. This is the point of Marxism. And you must understand that these are *your* children they are doing it to, so they can get what they want, which is total control over society."[9]

Lindsay warns that when you see terms such as comprehensive sex education (CSE) and social-emotional learning (SEL) at your child's school, your children are at risk. The Child Protection League agrees, warning that the goal of comprehensive sex education is to remove all "protective boundaries for children and teens, encouraging early sexual exploration in graphic detail. CSE uses porn-like images and graphic descriptions to teach children as young as 10 that all 'consensual' sexual activity is their 'right.'"[10]

A disturbing example of the CSE curriculum is a book called *It's Perfectly Normal*. Aimed at children ages ten and up, the book features graphic illustrations of various forms of sexual behavior, including intercourse.[11] That book may be in your child's school right now. By the time your children have read one of these soul-destroying books, it's too late. It cannot be unseen. The damage is done.

The assault on the innocence of children is just one more appalling feature of the Marxist, satanic assault on the family. Karl Marx himself, in part 2 of *The Communist Manifesto*, mocked his opponents for resisting an essential feature of Communism, the "abolition of the family." Even many radicals, he said, "flare up at this infamous proposal of the Communists."

The family must be abolished, Marx contended, in order to abolish the hated "bourgeois" class—the middle class, with its conventional, anti-revolutionary attitudes. The "bourgeois family," he wrote, is based "on capital, on private gain. In its completely developed form, this family exists only among the bourgeoisie."[12]

That's the Marxist agenda for the public schools: abolish the family—and the innocence of children.

If you are a parent or grandparent, I plead with you—if it is at all possible—*get your children or grandchildren out of the government school system immediately.* Get them into a private Christian school or a home-school co-op. If that's not possible, then get involved in your child's public school. Go to school board meetings. Visit your child's classroom. Talk to the teacher. Make sure you know exactly what is being taught to your children, what books are in the school library, and what sexual notions are being implanted in their pliable young souls.

It's hard to believe that people in the days of Noah imagined any sin as evil as this coordinated effort to destroy the souls of children. It seems to me that the times we live in must far exceed the wickedness of the world God judged with a flood. It should be no wonder, then, that an even more frightening fate lies ahead for this world.

EATING, DRINKING, MARRYING

Next, Jesus says: "For in the days before the flood, people were eating and drinking, marrying and giving in marriage, up to the day Noah entered the ark; and they knew nothing about what would happen until the flood came and took them all away. That is how it will be at the coming of the Son of Man" (Matt. 24:38–39).

There is nothing wrong with eating, drinking, and

marrying. That is not His point. He is saying that people in Noah's day were living as though life would go on as it always had. They were enjoying life and looking forward to the future. Young people were getting married and preparing to start families, completely unaware that the judgment of God was about to descend on the world in the form of a great flood to take them all away.

Food and drink were a popular obsession in the days of Noah—just as food and drink are an obsession of our culture today. When food and drink become our focus, our masters instead of our servants, then our priorities have turned upside down.

According to the US Census Bureau, Americans spent approximately $638 billion at restaurants and bars in the month of October 2021.[13] Let me put that in perspective. That is more money spent *in one month* in American restaurants and bars than the gross domestic product *for all of 2021* for many major nations, including Poland ($596.6 billion), Sweden ($541.5 billion), and Argentina ($389.1 billion).[14] Westerners in general, and Americans in particular, are obsessed with self-gratification and luxury.

Today, as in Noah's day, people enter marriage—and exit marriage—for purely selfish reasons. There's certainly nothing sinful about marriage. The institution of marriage and the strength of the family form the biblical cornerstone of a healthy society. The biblical design for a family is one man, one woman, and the children their love produces.

But sin distorts our attitude toward marriage and the family. In America today, the biblical blueprint for the family has broken down. Today, many people believe a marriage or a family can be anything we choose. A marriage may consist of two, three, or more people of any gender, without any boundaries. It's unlikely that even Noah's wicked culture redefined "marriage" and "family" in such extreme and ungodly ways as we have today. Clearly, judgment can't be far away.

"As it was in the days of Noah," said Jesus, "so it will be at the coming of the Son of Man."

Another characteristic of the days of Noah is mockery and scorn toward those who preach the truth of God. The apostle Peter wrote:

> If he [God] did not spare the ancient world when he brought the flood on its ungodly people, but protected Noah, a preacher of righteousness, and seven others...then the Lord knows how to rescue the godly from trials and to hold the unrighteous for punishment on the day of judgment.
>
> —2 PETER 2:5, 9

When Noah preached a message of righteousness and repentance to his neighbors, they mocked him, laughed at him, and ridiculed him. "Poor Noah," they said, "he's lost his mind. We have never seen rain, let alone a flood. We're living as we've always lived, as our forefathers lived—eating, drinking, marrying, enjoying life. Nothing bad happened to them. Nothing bad will happen to us." They ignored Noah's warnings to save themselves from the judgment to come.

One of the implications of Jesus' message is that we are to be like Noah. We are to invite people to receive Christ as Lord and Savior. We are to lovingly warn them of the coming judgment and show them from the Scriptures that only Jesus can save them from the coming judgment. Only Jesus can change their eternal destination. Only Jesus can deliver them from darkness to light, from sin to salvation, from death to life everlasting.

When we share Christ with others, we should not expect to be treated any better than Noah was. He faced mockery and rejection—and so will we. People will reject our message of righteousness and repentance, just as they rejected the word of Noah.

Knowing that our friends and neighbors and loved ones face judgment and terror should motivate us to share the good news of Jesus Christ. It should fill us with a sense of urgency. The Book of Revelation prophesies that in the day of judgment, the hearts of the people will be hardened. Instead of repenting of their sins, they will double down on them:

> The rest of mankind who were not killed by these plagues still did not repent of the work

of their hands; they did not stop worshiping demons, and idols of gold, silver, bronze, stone and wood—idols that cannot see or hear or walk. Nor did they repent of their murders, their magic arts, their sexual immorality or their thefts.

—REVELATION 9:20–21

"As it was in the days of Noah," said Jesus, "so it will be at the coming of the Son of Man." There is only one major difference between the days of Noah and that day of final judgment: the flood lasted for a short time—but God's judgment is for all eternity. Those who reject God's grace in this life will spend eternity in a pit of loneliness and regret.

THE BEST NEWS ON EARTH

How can loving Christians, full of Christlike compassion, withhold the good news from the people around them? How can we remain silent, knowing we have the best news on earth? How can we allow the people around us to go on living without Christ when just a few words from us might change their eternal destination?

No one knows the day or the hour when Jesus will return—but we must be ready for his return at any moment. Jesus predicted the destruction of Jerusalem and the temple. His prophecy was unbelievable, inconceivable to the disciples at the time—yet it was fulfilled precisely on time. Jesus also told His disciples about signs that would be fulfilled immediately before His return. Make no mistake, those signs will also be fulfilled precisely on time.

Some people say, "When things get really bad, I'll get right with God." My friend, this may be your one and only opportunity. You may never get another chance to come to Him. Later, when you think you might be ready, your mind and heart may be dazzled by material things, or you may be in the clutches of habits you can't break, or you may be in the company of people who will lead you away from God.

The notion that you can always get right with God at some later date is a trap Satan has set for you. Don't get caught in it. Come to Jesus now. He is waiting for you now.

At some future date, known only to the Father, Jesus will return suddenly and only those who are anticipating His return will rejoice on that day. Everyone else will despair. Jesus says:

> Two men will be in the field; one will be taken and the other left. Two women will be grinding with a hand mill; one will be taken and the other left. "Therefore keep watch, because you do not know on what day your Lord will come."
>
> —MATTHEW 24:40–42

This is how sudden and quick the end will be. Two people will be working together side by side. One will be taken to heaven, the other will stay behind to face the judgment.

"Therefore keep watch," Jesus says. Don't fall asleep. Be on guard. Keep watching for the Lord's return. Live with urgency in your heart and watch for His return.

Our Lord has challenged us with an imperative to live as Noah and his family lived—not as those who mocked Noah and his message of repentance. May we obey the Noah Imperative and seek refuge in Christ before God shuts the door.

Chapter 6

SUDDEN—AND UNEXPECTED

I ONCE HEARD A story about a coastal village in Scotland where, years ago, vessels would depart for months at a time. Sailors would leave wives and sweethearts to wait in the village for them to return.

On one occasion, a boat entered the harbor. Sailors lined the rail, gazing eagerly toward the dock where their loved ones stood watching for them.

The skipper raised his binoculars and spotted some familiar faces.

"I see Bill's wife, Mary," he said. "And there's Tom's beloved Ann. Oh, and there's David's Margaret."

All the sailors cheered and waved—except one. A sailor named Peter scanned the dock, eager for a glimpse of his wife, Jane. But she wasn't there. He

115

became anxious. Where was she? Was she sick? Had something happened to her?

The moment the boat docked, Peter leaped to the wharf and dashed up the street toward his cottage. He flung open the door, and there was his wife, Jane.

She ran to him, put her arms around him, and said, "Oh, Peter, I've been waiting for you."

"Aye," he said in a disappointed tone, "you've been *waiting*. But the other wives were *watching* for their husbands."

There is a great difference between *waiting* and *watching*. It's a difference that our Lord makes plain to us in His Olivet Discourse. Many of us in the church are *waiting* for the Lord's return. But how many of us are *watching* for His return?

JESUS, MUHAMMAD, AND BUDDHA

In August 2021 the *New York Times* ran a story headlined "The New Chief Chaplain at Harvard? An Atheist." The story opens with a brief history of Harvard University—that the institution was founded by Puritan colonists to train clergymen for the ministry, and that Harvard's motto was once "Truth for Christ and the Church." (Today, Harvard's motto is simply *Veritas*, Latin for "truth.") For the first seven decades of its existence, every president of Harvard was a minister of the gospel. Now, nearly four centuries after its founding, Harvard's chaplains' organization has elected an atheist, Greg Epstein, as its president. The *Times* explains:

> Mr. Epstein, 44, author of the book *Good Without God*, is a seemingly unusual choice for the role. He will coordinate the activities of more than 40 university chaplains, who lead the Christian, Jewish, Hindu, Buddhist, and other religious communities on campus. Yet many Harvard students—some raised in families of faith, others never quite certain how to label their religious identities—attest to the influence that Mr. Epstein has had on their spiritual lives.
>
> "There is a rising group of people who no longer identify with any religious tradition but still experience a real need for conversation and support around what it means to be a good human and live an ethical life," said Mr. Epstein.[1]

The fact that Harvard would appoint an atheist as its new chief chaplain is a shame but hardly a surprise. Harvard's slide into the abyss of apostasy has been an accomplished fact for many years. What is more disturbing is that so many young people—including, as the *Times* states, young people from "families of faith"—are rejecting the God of the Bible even though they are aware, on some level, of a God-shaped hole in their lives. People need much more than "conversation and support around what it means to be a good human." People need Jesus.

The dismal state of religion at Harvard is merely a reflection of religion across America. According to a recent survey, nearly 70 percent of Americans age eighteen to thirty-nine who identify as "Christians" hold a distinctly unbiblical, un-Christian view of faith and salvation. These self-described "Christians" disagree with Jesus' claim in John 14:6 that He is the only way to God—and they accept the apostate notion that Jesus, Muhammad, and Buddha all taught equally valid ways to God.[2]

The Lord makes it clear that a large-scale departure from the true faith, as we are now seeing throughout the church, indicates the nearness of His return. Those who are faithful to Jesus will not just *wait* for His return, but they will *watch* for His return. And when we see these signs that Jesus has given us, we will know that the end is near.

Earlier in Matthew 24, we saw Jesus make two contrasting statements, one beginning with "you know," the other beginning with "no one knows." Verse 33: "When you see all these things, *you know* that it is near, right at the door" (emphasis added). Verse 36: "But about that day or hour *no one knows*, not even the angels in heaven, nor the Son, but only the Father" (emphasis added). *We can know* the signs of the times, the signs that point to His imminent return—but *no one knows* the day or the hour of His return. We must not only wait, but we must keep watch and be ready, always prepared for the Lord's sudden and unexpected return.

Jesus teaches us that the time of His coming will also be a moment of sudden separation, when two people will be working side by side—one will be taken to meet the Lord, the other will be left behind to face an eternity without Christ. Those who claim that all religions lead to heaven will be in shock when they discover their error and loss.

Jesus makes it abundantly clear: On the day of judgment, not everyone will be saved. Many will be lost. The Old Testament prophet Malachi wrote of that day:

> "Surely the day is coming; it will burn like a furnace. All the arrogant and every evildoer will be stubble, and the day that is coming will set them on fire," says the LORD Almighty. "Not a root or a branch will be left to them. But for you who revere my name, the sun of righteousness will rise with healing in its rays. And you will go out and frolic like well-fed calves."
>
> —MALACHI 4:1–2

As He ushers in the kingdom of God, Jesus will separate the faithful from the unfaithful. He will consign all of humanity to one eternity or the other—either eternity with God or eternity apart from God.

Salvation—or Hell?

In Matthew 24:42–51 Jesus gives us two illustrations to show us how we should not only *wait* but expectantly *watch* for His return. Let's look closely at what He says to us about that day:

> Therefore keep watch, because you do not know on what day your Lord will come. But understand this: If the owner of the house had known at what time of night the thief was coming, he would have kept watch and would not have let his house be broken into. So you also must be ready, because the Son of Man will come at an hour when you do not expect him.
>
> Who then is the faithful and wise servant, whom the master has put in charge of the servants in his household to give them their food at the proper time? It will be good for that servant whose master finds him doing so when he returns. Truly I tell you, he will put him in charge of all his possessions. But suppose that servant is wicked and says to himself, "My master is staying away a long time," and he then begins to beat his fellow servants and to eat and drink with drunkards. The master of that servant will come on a day when he does not expect him and at an hour he is not aware of. He will cut him to pieces and assign him a place with the hypocrites, where there will be weeping and gnashing of teeth.

What are the two illustrations the Lord offers in this passage? First, there is the illustration of the thief in the night, who breaks into a house suddenly and without warning. Second, there is the illustration of the wise and faithful servant—whom Jesus contrasts with a foolish and wicked servant.

Jesus makes it clear that, on the day of His return, there will be a separation between believers and non-believers, between those who love the Lord and those who are not genuine Christians. There are some in the church who are preaching a strange doctrine that is completely opposed to the teachings of Jesus. This doctrine is called "universalism," the claim that everyone will be saved and no one will suffer eternal punishment, even after a lifetime of sin, rebellion, and rejecting the Lord.

People who profess to be "Christians" while teaching that God will not punish sin are in for a world of hurt. People who profess to be "Christians" while teaching that all religions lead to heaven are in for a world of hurt. Pastors and authors who profess to be "Christians" while leading many people into these demonic doctrines are in for a world of hurt.

Jesus sounded a warning that is clear and unambiguous: "Enter through the narrow gate. For wide is the gate and broad is the road that leads to destruction, and many enter through it. But small is the gate and narrow the road that leads to life, and only a few find it" (Matt. 7:13–14). There's no wiggle room in those words for universalism or any other heresy. Anyone who fails to take Jesus at His word is in for a world of hurt.

As we have already seen, Jesus teaches in the Olivet Discourse that two will be in the same place together—they might be members of the same family, or coworkers in the same office, or co-laborers in the same field, or roommates in the same dorm, or neighbors in the same condominium complex. They might even be members of the same church, sitting side by side in the same pew. If one is a genuine believer and the other is not, then one will go to heaven—and the other will face judgment and hell.

This is what Jesus is saying to us in these verses. The full weight of the Lord's warning should drive us to search our souls. Jesus seeks to disabuse us of the heretical teaching that has become so widespread, both inside the church and out—the notion that everyone will go to heaven.

We frequently hear people substituting their own wishful thinking in place of the clear warnings of Jesus. They say, "I just can't believe that a God of love would send anyone to hell." The reality, of course, is that people choose hell by their disobedience to God's truth.

No one in the Bible spoke more about hell than Jesus Himself. He spoke more about hell than He spoke about heaven—and He described hell in the most dire and vivid terms. Most of what we know about hell and judgment comes from the lips of our Savior.

One of the clearest examples of Jesus' warnings

against the awfulness of hell is in Matthew 24:50–51, where He says, "The master of that servant will come on a day when he does not expect him and at an hour he is not aware of. He will cut him to pieces and assign him a place with the hypocrites, where there will be weeping and gnashing of teeth."

Jesus paid for our salvation with His blood, and He warns us that not everyone will be saved. Many will be lost. Life is not a contest in which everyone gets a trophy. Life is a journey of choices, and the choices we make determine whether we have been faithful or unfaithful to God. On that day when Jesus returns, God will separate the faithful from the unfaithful.

As you read these words, I urge you to ask yourself, "Am I in the faith?" Being born into a Christian family will not save you. Attending church will not save you. Having many Christian friends will not save you.

Salvation is not hereditary. Salvation is not something you can absorb by osmosis through hearing sermons or listening to Christian music. Salvation is an individual submission of your will to the will of God, an act of repentance and receiving by faith the free gift of salvation.

A Thief in the Night

The second illustration our Lord uses in this passage is that of a thief. It's fascinating and ironic that our righteous Lord compares Himself here to a thief. But the reason this is such an apt analogy is that only the image of a thief accurately conveys the suddenness and unexpectedness of the Lord's second coming.

In our own culture, thieves often operate during the daytime while people are at work. But in the ancient Middle East, thieves worked almost exclusively at night because there was usually someone home all day. In order to enter someone's house to steal, thieves had to work at night while their victims slept. The thief would silently approach a house under the cover of darkness and gently test the doors and windows to see if the owner had forgotten to lock them. Once inside, he had to do his work quickly and escape before anyone woke up.

Thieves do not announce they are coming. Thieves don't make noise and wake people up. The arrival of the thief is silent, sudden, and unexpected. He comes and he leaves before anyone is any the wiser.

That is what the return of the Lord will be like. That's why we see the Lord's return portrayed with this same image again and again in Scripture: "For you know very well that the day of the Lord will come like a thief in the night" (1 Thess. 5:2). "But the day of the Lord will come like a thief" (2 Pet. 3:10). And Jesus, speaking to the church in Sardis in John's vision, said: "Remember, therefore, what you have received and heard; hold it fast, and repent. But if you do not wake up, I will come like a thief, and you will not know at what time I will come to you" (Rev. 3:3).

Question: What does a thief come to steal? Answer: That which is most valuable.

That's why people put their most prized possessions in safety deposit boxes in banks. Banks have alarms and steel bars that are intended to make those possessions theft-proof. People don't leave their most precious possessions lying around for someone to come and steal.

What is your most valuable possession? Your one and only irreplaceable soul.

That's why Jesus asks, "What good will it be for someone to gain the whole world, yet forfeit their soul? Or what can anyone give in exchange for their soul?" (Matt. 16:26).

Some people become obsessed with their material possessions, whether money or gold or jewelry or investments or their home or car. They worry and fret about something bad happening to their possessions. But which is more precious—your "stuff" or your soul?

If your soul is your most prized and irreplaceable possession, shouldn't you make sure it is protected from all harm? Once you know your soul is safe, you can sleep like a baby. Once your soul is safe, you have no worries or fears about the end-time. You have no anxiety about the labor pains of history. While everyone around you is panicking, you have perfect peace.

Why? Because your most prized possession is in the Lord's safety deposit box. Because we know our most precious possession is secure in His care, we

are motivated to live for Him out of abundant grati-
tude. We are at peace with God. Our spiritual bags are
packed. We are ready to go at any moment. We are not
merely waiting for the Lord's return. We are eagerly
watching, expecting, and hoping.

"Therefore keep watch," Jesus said, "because you
do not know on what day your Lord will come....So
you also must be ready, because the Son of Man will
come at an hour when you do not expect him" (Matt.
24:42, 44).

Jesus gives us these illustrations, these powerful
word pictures, because He wants us to understand—
and be ready for—the sudden nature of His return.
His earlier word pictures—the flood of Noah and the
image of two people working in a field—also remind
us that we cannot be saved merely by being close to
someone who is saved.

Each of us must make the decision to submit and
commit our lives to Christ. We must take care that our
most prized possession is safeguarded and protected
when that day comes like a thief in the night.

Jesus has solemnly warned us. Have we taken His
warning seriously? Will we be prepared when that day
comes?

A CONTRAST OF SERVANTS

Finally, our Lord shows us how we should wait and
watch for His return through the illustration of two
servants—the faithful servant and the unfaithful

servant, the watchful servant and the oblivious servant. The faithful servant is ready at all times—and he keeps busy while he waits. He is faithful in serving, doing, and giving.

In verses 45–46 Jesus says, "Who then is the faithful and wise servant, whom the master has put in charge of the servants in his household to give them their food at the proper time? It will be good for that servant whose master finds him doing so when he returns." What is the faithful servant's motivation for serving? He knows his master is returning and he is eager to receive his master's approval.

In Luke 19 Jesus tells the story of the master who gives ten servants money to invest. He tells his servants, "Put this money to work until I come back" (v. 13). The English Standard Version translates this command, "Engage in business until I come." The King James Version renders it, "Occupy till I come." In each version the meaning is clear: The servants are not simply to wait for the master's return. They are to be busy doing the master's work, increasing the master's investment.

How does Jesus expect you and me to "occupy" until He comes? How are we to "engage in business" and increase His investment until He returns?

We are to be busy working, serving, and witnessing. We are to live righteously. We are to minister to others until He comes. We are to advance the kingdom. We are to win souls to Jesus.

In 2010 famed illusionist Penn Jillette—the talking

half of the magic team Penn and Teller—recorded a YouTube video in which he told the story of an experience he had after a stage performance. Penn is widely known as an atheist, which makes the story he tells all the more astonishing.

After the show, Penn was signing autographs when he recognized a man who had been in the audience for his magic act. The man was, in Penn's words, "a big guy," and about the same age as Penn. He walked up and said, "I really liked the show." He was very complimentary, and he handed Penn a pocket New Testament and Psalms.

Reflecting on their conversation, Penn said, "It was really wonderful. I believe he knew that I was an atheist, but he was not defensive. He was truly complimentary, and it didn't seem like empty flattery. He was really kind and nice and sane, and he looked me in the eyes and talked to me."

Then Penn made a statement that, coming from an atheist, is truly amazing: "I've always said that I don't respect [Christians] who believe strongly, but who don't proselytize [that is, who don't tell others about Jesus Christ]. If you believe that there's a heaven and hell, and you believe that people could be going to hell, and you don't think it's really worth telling people this because it would make it socially awkward—how much do you have to hate somebody to not say anything? How much do you have to hate somebody to believe that everlasting life is possible and not tell them that?...

"This guy was a really good guy. He was polite and honest and sane, and he cared enough about me to proselytize and give me a New Testament, in which he had written a little note to me, 'I liked your show' and some phone numbers and an email address if I wanted to get in touch.

"Now, I know there's no God, and one polite person living his life right doesn't change that. But I'll tell you, he was a very, very good man. That's really important. With that kind of goodness, it's okay to have that deep a disagreement....That was a good man who gave me that book."[3]

The Lord Jesus says that we are to preach the good news of the kingdom to everyone around us. And as amazing as it sounds, one of the world's leading atheists agrees. You and I have the good news of salvation. Let's not keep it to ourselves. Let's share it with others and win as many as possible to eternal life in Christ.

What does Jesus mean when He says that the "faithful and wise servant" has the responsibility of giving the servants their food "at the proper time"? What kind of food is Jesus talking about?

He is charging us to feed each other spiritually with the Word of God. We are to see that our brothers and sisters in the church are spiritually nourished with the Bread of Life.

Unfaithful servants feed on junk food while lazily wasting time. As Jesus says in Matthew 24:48–49, "But suppose that servant is wicked and says to himself, 'My master is staying away a long time,' and he then begins to beat his fellow servants and to eat and drink with drunkards."

Instead of serving one another the good food of God's Word, unfaithful servants spread the poison of criticism, bitterness, complaints, faithlessness, and self-ishness throughout the church. They make the body of Christ sick with their habitual sins and their attacks against others in the church.

Jesus warns us that the unfaithful servant is destined for destruction. In verses 50–51, He says, "The master of that servant will come on a day when he does not expect him and at an hour he is not aware of. He will cut him to pieces and assign him a place with the hyp-ocrites, where there will be weeping and gnashing of teeth."

This is a warning we dare not ignore—a call to sober self-examination, repentance, and total submission to Christ.

OVERCOMING THE DEMONIC STRATEGY

The apostle Paul, in the last letter he wrote before going to his execution, told his young disciple Timothy:

> There will be terrible times in the last days. People will be lovers of themselves, lovers of money, boastful, proud, abusive, disobedient to their parents, ungrateful, unholy, without love, unforgiving, slanderous, without self-control,

brutal, not lovers of the good, treacherous, rash,
conceited, lovers of pleasure rather than lovers
of God—having a form of godliness but denying
its power. Have nothing to do with such people.
—2 TIMOTHY 3:1–5

Isn't that an uncannily accurate description of the days in which we live? Our culture is saturated with narcissism, arrogance, greed, boastfulness, pride, brutality, and hedonism. The young have no respect for their parents. Our political system, our news media, and our social media are all about slandering people, destroying reputations, and destroying lives. Even in the church, we see an abandonment of biblical truth in favor of worldly social agendas.

The apostle Paul also wrote, "The Spirit clearly says that in later times some will abandon the faith and follow deceiving spirits and things taught by demons" (1 Tim. 4:1). It's important that we understand that many of the false and deceptive notions that are being taught in our society and even in the church come straight out of hell. These are doctrines of demons.

There is an old fable that makes an important point for our times. Three apprentice demons were being trained in wickedness and deception by an old devil. The devil asked the three apprentices, "How will you deceive human beings and seduce them into hell?"

The first apprentice demon said, "I will whisper to them, 'There is no God.' I will conquer them by turning them into atheists."

The old devil said, "Fool! That approach almost never works! Even the atheist, in the secret chambers of his own soul, knows there is a God."

The second apprentice demon said, "I will whisper to them, 'There is no hell.' I will conquer them by convincing them they need not fear the final judgment."

The old devil said, "Fool! That approach won't work. They may try to deceive themselves, but their conscience testifies that there is right and there is wrong, there is heaven and there is hell."

The third apprentice demon said, "I will whisper to them, 'There is plenty of time to repent and believe. Why hurry?'"

The old devil said, "Correct! That is how you will conquer them. Go out, my apprentice, and ruin eternity for millions of human beings."

If you think you have plenty of time to get right with God, if you think you'll have many opportunities to commit your life to Jesus Christ, if you think there's no reason to hurry—you have bought Satan's lie. Your most precious possession—your eternal soul—is in great danger. I urge you, I beg you, do not make this mistake. Do not let the satanic strategy ruin your entire eternity. Today, this very moment, might be the only opportunity you'll have. It may not come again.

Say yes to Jesus. Receive the gift of eternal life while there is still time.

Chapter 7

THE GREAT SEPARATION

F YOU DO an internet search asking such questions as, "What does the Bible teach about hell?" some of the first few results will be from false teachers. Here are the titles of webpages that popped up at the top of my search: "Hell Is Not a Biblical Concept." "Jesus Christ Did Not Teach or Believe in Hell." "There Is No Hell in the Bible." "Heaven and Hell Are 'Not What Jesus Preached,' Religion Scholar Says." It is shocking that so many of these false teachers will look you in the eye and deny what is plainly printed on the pages of God's Word.

Jesus spoke more about heaven and hell than any other preacher or prophet in the Bible. Jesus spoke more about hell than He spoke about heaven. Yet He always talked about judgment in the most caring and compassionate language. Why? Because He was pleading with people to repent, to receive the free gift of salvation, and to escape the wrath to come. Jesus wept over Jerusalem because the people's rejection of Him would result in judgment. And He weeps over every human soul who rejects Him and incurs the coming judgment.

We come now to the second half of the longest answer Jesus ever gave to a question from His disciples. The Olivet Discourse, remember, is the second longest sermon Jesus delivered, next to the Sermon on the Mount (Matt. 5–7). The sheer length and depth of Jesus' reply to the disciples in Matthew 24–25 speaks volumes about the importance Jesus placed on the second coming. He wants us to live in a daily sense of hope and expectation. He wants us to be prepared for His return.

As we wait for Him to come back for us, Jesus warns us not to be deceived by false messiahs and false preachers and their deceptive teachings. He pleads with us to repent and accept God's plan of salvation. He pleads with us to take refuge in Him from the wrath to come.

In Matthew 25, the closing section of the Olivet Discourse, Jesus delivers three crucial parables to illustrate His compassionate yet sober warning of the endtime. They are "The Parable of the Ten Virgins," "The Parable of the Bags of Gold," and "The Sheep and the Goats." The common theme of these three parables is clear: "Therefore keep watch, because you do not know the day or the hour" (v. 13).

THE TEN VIRGINS

The first parable is "The Parable of the Ten Virgins." Here Jesus tells a profound story about being prepared to meet the Lord.

In school students take tests to determine whether or not they have prepared themselves to succeed in a given subject. Those who pass the test have prepared themselves, and those who fail the test have not prepared themselves.

Outwardly, the students in a classroom might appear to be roughly the same. They are all about the same age, they all have the same teacher and attend the same school, and they all have the same amount of time to study. But the test will separate those who have prepared themselves from those who have not.

"The Parable of the Ten Virgins" is the story of a test. It's the story of ten young women who all seem very much alike. They're all about the same age, attending the same wedding in the same town—yet they are about to undergo a test that will separate the prepared from the unprepared.

This parable presents a picture of Christians who all outwardly look alike, but are not alike. Some are prepared to meet the Lord and some are not. Some are merely "professing Christians." They outwardly claim to be "Christians," but their words and actions belie those claims. They are partakers in the great apostasy, the great falling away from faith that Jesus said would take place immediately before His return.

This story urges us to examine ourselves, asking, "Am I prepared to pass the test? If Jesus were to return today, or if I were to die today, would I be ready to meet the Lord face to face?"

Theologians differ over whether the Lord's return will take place before the great tribulation, or during, or after. I honestly don't care whether I will have to go through the tribulation or if the Lord will remove me and His church before the tribulation begins. It makes no difference to me who the Antichrist is. Many Christians focus intensely on these matters, but they do not interest me.

I have one concern regarding the end-time: Am I prepared to meet the Lord when He returns? That is my sole concern because that is the issue the Lord highlights in The Parable of the Ten Virgins. Jesus says:

> At that time the kingdom of heaven will be like ten virgins who took their lamps and went out to meet the bridegroom. Five of them were foolish and five were wise. The foolish ones took their lamps but did not take any oil with them. The wise ones, however, took oil in jars along with their lamps. The bridegroom was a long time in coming, and they all became drowsy and fell asleep.

At midnight the cry rang out: "Here's the bridegroom! Come out to meet him!"

Then all the virgins woke up and trimmed their lamps. The foolish ones said to the wise, "Give us some of your oil; our lamps are going out."

"No," they replied, "there may not be enough for both us and you. Instead, go to those who sell oil and buy some for yourselves."

But while they were on their way to buy the oil, the bridegroom arrived. The virgins who were ready went in with him to the wedding banquet. And the door was shut.

Later the others also came. "Lord, Lord," they said, "open the door for us!"

But he replied, "Truly I tell you, I don't know you."

Therefore keep watch, because you do not know the day or the hour.

—MATTHEW 25:1–13

The wise virgins demonstrate their wisdom by living their lives as if the bridegroom could return any moment. They are prepared. They have oil in their lamps. The foolish virgins, on the other hand, are unprepared. They have neglected the most important mission in life: watching and waiting for the bridegroom.

When the virgins hear the shout—"The bridegroom

is here!"—the wise virgins are prepared. But the foolish virgins say, "Oops! We have lamps but we have no oil!"

To translate this story to the church today, the foolish virgins represent those who say, "I'm a Christian," but they reject the claims of Christ. "I have religion," but their religion has no power. "I have a religious tradition," but they do not have the life of Christ. "I have church membership," but they don't have salvation.

You cannot inherit salvation. You cannot earn salvation. You receive only enough salvation for yourself, just as the wise virgins had only enough oil for their own lamps. Some people think they can say a prayer at the last moment, as they are dying or as the last trumpet is sounding, and they will be saved. But many will be just like the foolish virgins who didn't think to buy oil until it was too late.

In ancient Israel there were three stages to a wedding. Stage one: the parents agree on the marriage of their son and daughter. Step two: the betrothal or engagement period, which is as legally binding as marriage itself. Step three: the wedding feast and celebration, which solemnifies the marriage. Between the betrothal and the wedding feast, the groom busily builds an addition to his father's house for his bride—and he prepares the addition for the purpose of welcoming his bride.

You and I are in stage two of our relationship with Christ—the betrothal stage. The Father has agreed to the marriage of Jesus Christ and His bride, the church.

We have entered into a binding engagement period, and Jesus, our Bridegroom, is preparing an eternal home for us. We await the future celebration—the wedding feast of the Lamb that John writes about in Revelation 19:6–9. When our eternal home is ready, Jesus will return, and there will be music, dancing, and feasting, along with shouts: "The Bridegroom is here!"

In the Parable of the Ten Virgins, Jesus is telling us that, at His first coming, He invited whosoever will to come and take part in the great marriage celebration. He is betrothing all who will accept His invitation. But He will betroth only those who love Him enough to watch and wait for His return.

There will be some who are invited, but who have not loved Him. There will be some who admire the Bridegroom, but were too foolish to surrender everything to Him. There will be some who have joined a local church, who see themselves as good religious people—but they are not part of the true church of Jesus Christ. They have never been born again. Some even wear the vestments of the clergy—but they do not wear the robe of the righteousness of Jesus Christ.

The foolish virgins in the Lord's parable are not atheists or pagans or hedonists. They do not hate Christians or mock the gospel. No, the foolish virgins represent people who are inside the church! They represent people who claim to be Christians, who attend church every Sunday.

Outwardly, there is no way to distinguish the foolish

virgins from the wise. Both the foolish and the wise have heard the invitation to the wedding. Both have responded to the invitation. Both are members of the wedding party (the visible church).

But on the day when the Bridegroom comes to claim His bride, the foolish will be separated from the wise by one single fact: the wise are prepared; the foolish are not. Once the Bridegroom appears, all similarities disappear. The wise have oil for their lamps; they have the Holy Spirit living in them; they have been born again; they are living for the Lord. The foolish have no oil and no inner transformation.

The oil is a symbol of being completely, unreservedly sold out to Jesus. Do you have oil in your lamp? Do you have a burning love for Jesus at the center of your life? Do you long for the day of the Lord's return? Do live and give and serve in anticipation of that great day? Are you wise—or foolish?

When the door is shut, it is shut forever. The time is now. Today is the day of salvation.

Anthony Ashley Cooper, the Seventh Earl of Shaftesbury, was a great English leader who reformed child labor laws, opposed opium trafficking, and helped lead the evangelical movement in the Church of England. He once said, "I do not think that in the last forty years I have ever lived one conscious hour that was not influenced by the thought of our Lord's return."[1]

That is the mindset of a wise follower of Christ. That is the meaning of the Parable of the Ten Virgins.

THE BAGS OF GOLD

Jesus also tells "The Parable of the Bags of Gold," a story about three servants who were given different amounts of money to manage:

> Again, it will be like a man going on a journey, who called his servants and entrusted his wealth to them. To one he gave five bags of gold, to another two bags, and to another one bag, each according to his ability. Then he went on his journey. The man who had received five bags of gold went at once and put his money to work and gained five bags more. So also, the one with two bags of gold gained two more. But the man who had received one bag went off, dug a hole in the ground and hid his master's money.
>
> After a long time the master of those servants returned and settled accounts with them. The man who had received five bags of gold brought the other five. "Master," he said, "you entrusted me with five bags of gold. See, I have gained five more."
>
> His master replied, "Well done, good and faithful servant! You have been faithful with a few things; I will put you in charge of many things. Come and share your master's happiness!"
>
> The man with two bags of gold also came.

"Master," he said, "you entrusted me with two bags of gold; see, I have gained two more."

His master replied, "Well done, good and faithful servant! You have been faithful with a few things; I will put you in charge of many things. Come and share your master's happiness!"

Then the man who had received one bag of gold came. "Master," he said, "I knew that you are a hard man, harvesting where you have not sown and gathering where you have not scattered seed. So I was afraid and went out and hid your gold in the ground. See, here is what belongs to you."

His master replied, "You wicked, lazy servant! So you knew that I harvest where I have not sown and gather where I have not scattered seed? Well then, you should have put my money on deposit with the bankers, so that when I returned I would have received it back with interest.

"So take the bag of gold from him and give it to the one who has ten bags. For whoever has will be given more, and they will have an abundance. Whoever does not have, even what they have will be taken from them. And throw that worthless servant outside, into the darkness, where there will be weeping and gnashing of teeth."

—MATTHEW 25:14–30

You have also heard this story referred to as "The Parable of the Talents." Though the NIV uses the term "bags of gold" for clarity, some Bible translations use the term "talent," from the Greek word *talanton*, meaning a scale and balance. A talent was a unit of weight equal to about eighty pounds. A talent of gold would have paid for about twenty years' worth of labor from a day laborer—so the master in this story was entrusting a huge amount of wealth in the hands of these servants.

The servant who received five bags of gold invested his money, put his money to work—and doubled it. The servant who received two bags of gold also invested his money and doubled it. But the man who had received one bag of gold simply buried it in a hole in the ground. The money was not invested and earned no interest.

When the master returned, he demanded his money and the interest it had earned. The servant who had buried the gold said that he knew the master was "a hard man," adding, "So I was afraid and went out and hid your gold."

The master responded by ordering the "wicked, lazy servant" to be thrown outside "into the darkness, where there will be weeping and gnashing of teeth."

Was the master unfair? No. He knew the hearts of his three servants. He knew how each one would respond to his assignment. This is evident by the amounts of gold entrusted to each servant. He knew that his most responsible and industrious servant would do an excellent job of investing five bags of gold. He knew that the second servant, while not as capable as the first, could still be trusted to wisely invest the money. As for the third servant, the master had him sized up pretty well, too.

Why didn't the lazy servant put his bag of gold to good use to benefit the master? Why didn't he make an effort to bring glory to the master? His only excuse: "I was afraid." He allowed fear to keep him from carrying out his most important assignment. Because he was ruled by fear, he disobeyed his master. So the master fired the servant and threw him out.

The lazy servant lost the confidence of the master—and he lost the opportunity to ever serve the master again.

Jesus, of course, is the Master. Before He left this earth, He gave us a task, which is the Great Commission. He commanded us to spread the gospel to all the nations of the world, to invest His good news in the lives of the people around us. When the Master returns, He expects to receive a huge return on investment.

What will we say to Him when He demands an accounting for the way we have used our lives? Will we present to Him the saved souls of the many people we have witnessed to over a lifetime as His servants? Or will we have to say, "I was afraid—so I didn't witness to anyone, and I simply hid Your good news in a hole in the ground"?

Don't let fear rob you of the joy of serving Jesus by sharing the good news with others. You have a treasure worth more than all the gold in the world. Invest it. Share it. Grow it. Use it to expand the kingdom of heaven.

Live your life in such a way that you will never have to stand before the Master and confess, "I was afraid."

The Sheep and the Goats

The third parable of the Lord pictures final judgment as a time when God separates the "sheep" from the "goats," the saved from the lost:

> When the Son of Man comes in his glory, and all the angels with him, he will sit on his glorious throne. All the nations will be gathered before him, and he will separate the people one from another as a shepherd separates the sheep from the goats. He will put the sheep on his right and the goats on his left.
>
> Then the King will say to those on his right, "Come, you who are blessed by my Father; take your inheritance, the kingdom prepared for you since the creation of the world. For I was hungry and you gave me something to eat, I was thirsty and you gave me something to drink, I was a stranger and you invited me in, I needed clothes and you clothed me, I was sick and you looked after me, I was in prison and you came to visit me."
>
> Then the righteous will answer him, "Lord, when did we see you hungry and feed you, or thirsty and give you something to drink? When

did we see you a stranger and invite you in, or
needing clothes and clothe you? When did we
see you sick or in prison and go to visit you?"

The King will reply, "Truly I tell you, whatever you did for one of the least of these brothers
and sisters of mine, you did for me."

Then he will say to those on his left, "Depart
from me, you who are cursed, into the eternal
fire prepared for the devil and his angels. For I
was hungry and you gave me nothing to eat, I
was thirsty and you gave me nothing to drink,
I was a stranger and you did not invite me in, I
needed clothes and you did not clothe me, I was
sick and in prison and you did not look after me."

They also will answer, "Lord, when did we see
you hungry or thirsty or a stranger or needing
clothes or sick or in prison, and did not help
you?"

He will reply, "Truly I tell you, whatever you
did not do for one of the least of these, you did
not do for me."

Then they will go away to eternal punishment,
but the righteous to eternal life.

—MATTHEW 25:31–46

In the Middle East you often find that goats and
sheep graze together on the same pastures. Both are
four-legged creatures that eat grass—but that's about
all they have in common. Goats and sheep exhibit
different behaviors. They have different habits and
temperaments.

Sheep are docile and compliant creatures. They love to follow the shepherd. They are easily guided and herded.

Goats, on the other hand, are rambunctious and unruly animals. They are stubborn and independent. They often go their own way instead of following the leadership of the shepherd. They are never contented, and are often butting heads with each other. Goats delight in misleading and aggravating the sheep.

Though sheep and goats can share the same pastures during the day, before nightfall the shepherd makes sure that the sheep are separated from the goats. Why? Because the sheep would never be able to rest in the company of goats.

From a distance, sheep and goats look alike and sound alike. But up close, the differences between them are unmistakable.

That's why Jesus often speaks of His sheep—not His goats. He never said, "My goats listen to my voice." No. He said, "My sheep listen to my voice; I know them, and they follow me" (John 10:27).

Why doesn't Jesus use goats for this metaphor? Because goats would never obey the voice of the shepherd. Sheep recognize the voice of the shepherd—but to goats, one voice is as good as another. To the goats, one shepherd is as good as another. To goats, all roads lead to the same destination. Goats have no discernment, no loyalty, no desire to follow the shepherd. They can't tell truth from lies.

Just as a shepherd separates the sheep from the goats at nightfall, on the day of judgment the Good Shepherd, the judge of the world, will divide humanity into His "sheep" and the "goats" who rejected Him and went their own way.

The "goats" may have been very religious people—but religion is not the same as a relationship with the Good Shepherd. The "goats" might have done many good deeds in their lifetime—but good deeds are no substitute for a saving relationship with Jesus. The "goats" may have bought the lie that God will let everyone into heaven—but that's because they have rejected the clear warnings of Jesus Himself.

Those who thought their religion or their good deeds qualified them as sheep will be devastated to discover that they were "goats" after all. You might ask, "But what about all the good deeds Jesus spoke of—feeding the hungry and sheltering strangers and ministering to the needy, sick, and imprisoned? Isn't Jesus saying that good works are a qualification for salvation?"

No, the good deeds Jesus speaks of are the *result* of salvation—not the *reason* the "sheep" have been saved. Good deeds are the *fruit* of salvation, not the *root* of salvation. The righteous were not saved *by* their good works, but were saved *for* a life of good works.

Neither the sheep nor the goats seem surprised to find themselves where they are. Yet they are clearly surprised to discover *why* they are there. They had been judged according to how they have treated Jesus

Christ—that is, how they have treated His children and those who belong to Him.

In this parable, Jesus shines a bright light on the four dimensions of the coming judgment:

1. The person—Jesus Christ, the judge of all the earth

2. The place—the great and glorious throne of judgment

3. The process—the separation of the saved from the lost

4. The pronouncement—The unsaved, the unbelieving, those who rejected the Lord and despised His followers will be consigned to eternal punishment.

1. The Person

The person who is central to the second half of the Olivet Discourse is Jesus Christ, the judge of all the earth. Jesus Himself will judge the human race. When the religious leaders persecuted Him for healing on the Sabbath, He told them: "For just as the Father raises the dead and gives them life, even so the Son gives life to whom he is pleased to give it. Moreover, the Father judges no one, but has entrusted all judgment to the Son, that all may honor the Son just as they honor the Father. Whoever does not honor the Son does not honor the Father, who sent him" (John 5:21–23).

This is the first time Jesus referred to Himself as King. Throughout His earthly ministry Jesus talked about the kingdom of God—but He rarely spoke of Himself as King. He probably wanted to avoid misunderstandings among His followers who expected Him to set up an earthly kingdom. Yet in this contentious encounter with the religious leaders who opposed Him, He boldly declared Himself to be both King and judge.

In His earthly life, the Son of Man lived and died in humility. One day, He will return and rule with a rod of iron. The One who died on the cross is none other than the King of heaven and the judge of all the earth. That is why only those who belong to King Jesus, who worship King Jesus, who bow to King Jesus, who serve King Jesus, who love King Jesus, and who obey King Jesus will enter His glorious kingdom. They will be citizens of the kingdom of God.

There are false teachers in the church who acknowledge that Jesus is the Son of Man, a wise teacher who taught us how to live in harmony with others. But they refuse to believe in Him as the Son of God, the King, and the coming judge.

Many people seem amazed at the notion that Jesus would come again in all His majestic power as the King and judge of the human race. But why is that amazing?

We shouldn't be astonished that Jesus the Son will return in all His power and glory. Rather, we should be astonished that He ever came in humility and grace to die for us and offer us the gift of salvation.

We shouldn't be amazed that He will judge sinners. Rather, we should be amazed that He offers pardon and forgiveness for those who trust in Him.

When will judgment begin? The moment Jesus appears—immediately after the sun and the moon darken, immediately after the earthquakes and tsunamis shake and drown the land, immediately after those who have rejected Him begin to weep and mourn, immediately after people begin to die of fright. Judgment will begin when He comes with power and great glory, as John foresaw in the Book of Revelation:

> Then I saw a great white throne and him who was seated on it. The earth and the heavens fled from his presence, and there was no place for them. And I saw the dead, great and small, standing before the throne, and books were opened. Another book was opened, which is the book of life. The dead were judged according to what they had done as recorded in the books.
> —REVELATION 20:11–12

How will your life be judged on that day? Is your name written in the Book of Life?

2. THE PLACE

The place of judgment is that great and glorious white throne.

When the Virgin Mary discovered that she was pregnant, the angel said to her, "You will conceive and give birth to a son, and you are to call him Jesus. He will be great and will be called the Son of the Most High. The Lord God will give him the throne of his father David, and he will reign over Jacob's descendants forever; his kingdom will never end" (Luke 1:31–33).

God will give Jesus the throne of David from which He will rule over an eternal kingdom. It will be a throne of authority—and of judgment. On that day, at that place, it will be too late for those who have rejected Jesus as Lord and Savior.

That is why the hour of repentance is *this* hour and the place of repentance is *this* place, wherever you happen to be right now. For the day of His return will be a day of separation. As the prophet Joel foretold:

> The LORD will roar from Zion and thunder from Jerusalem; the earth and the heavens will tremble. But the LORD will be a refuge for his people, a stronghold for the people of Israel.
>
> —JOEL 3:16

Every person from every tribe and every land will be judged. Every person from every generation and from every nation will stand before the judgment seat of Christ.

3. The Process

Genuine believers are the true sheep of Christ. Because genuine believers are filled with the Holy Spirit, they naturally love and serve, give of themselves, sacrifice themselves, and reach out to people in need. They don't even realize what they are doing, because good deeds are simply the fruit of their new nature.

The goats, on the other hand, live for themselves. Even their good works are mostly "virtue signaling," showing off how much they care about this or that cause. As the apostle Paul said, those who do good works without being motivated by a Christlike love and compassion are like a "resounding gong or a clanging cymbal" (1 Cor. 13:1).

The process of the Lord's judgment will be very simple: sheep to the right, goats to the left. Those who are His on one side, those who are not His on the other. Those who had a genuine relationship with the Good Shepherd on one side, those who never knew Him on the other.

The word picture of sheep and goats was familiar imagery to the disciples. If you are a city slicker like me, you rarely ever see a sheep or a goat. You may need to have this word picture explained to you. But the application is very simple: if you have placed your complete trust in the Lord Jesus for your salvation, if you have humbly asked Him to save you from your sins, you are a sheep.

If, however, you are full of your own ideas of who God is, if you think God has an obligation to let everybody into heaven, or if you think you are entitled to eternal life because your "good deeds" outweigh your "bad deeds," then you are a goat. You have rejected God's plan of salvation. You have rejected His Son, the Lord Jesus. You have decided that you don't need Jesus; you can save yourself. That is stubborn, self-willed, goat-headed thinking.

But here's the good news: the day of judgment is not here yet. It's just around the corner, it's at the door—but it's not here yet. You may have only the next few moments, but there is still time. Right now, you can confess that you are a sinner and ask Jesus to come into your life and save you.

Even if you are a goat right now, you can still become a sheep.

4. The Pronouncement

Jesus concludes the parable of the sheep and goats in Matthew 25:46: "Then they will go away to eternal punishment, but the righteous to eternal life."

This is the pronouncement. On the day of judgment, the goats will be consigned to eternal punishment. Why? Because of their unbelief. Because they failed to recognize Jesus as the only way to the Father. Because they have failed to serve Him in obedience. Because, as unbelievers, they are unfit for His kingdom. Because they have persecuted and mocked Jesus' followers. Because they have belittled Jesus' own claim to be King.

Jesus describes hell as "eternal punishment" and "the eternal fire prepared for the devil and his angels" (v. 41).

It is a punishment from which there is no escape, no relief, no rest.

By contrast, those who have accepted Jesus' payment on the cross, who have acknowledged their sin and desperation apart from Christ, who have gratefully accepted His forgiveness—they will inherit eternal joy in God's presence. The contrast between heaven and hell could not be more stark.

The time to prepare for the judgment is now. As Jesus said:

> Therefore keep watch because you do not know when the owner of the house will come back— whether in the evening, or at midnight, or when the rooster crows, or at dawn. If he comes suddenly, do not let him find you sleeping. What I say to you, I say to everyone: "Watch!"
>
> —MARK 13:35–37

There are genuine Christians in this world, and there are "cultural Christians"; there are sheep, and there are goats. Genuine Christians have submitted their will to the will of God. Their relationship with Christ is central to their thinking, their decision-making, and their behavior. They spend time each day talking to God and reading His Word. Their personal relationship with Jesus is central, not peripheral, to their lives.

If you think you may be a "cultural Christian," what Jesus in this parable calls a "goat," you can change that right now. Submit your life to the Lord Jesus

Christ—today, right now. Make sure you have nothing to fear when Jesus returns—and make sure you live forever with Him.

Chapter 8

TRUE SECURITY IN A COLLAPSING WORLD

A GERMAN FRIEND, WHO is more than a hundred years old, once told me about life in Germany after that nation's defeat in World War I. After four years of war, from 1914 to 1918, the German people were weary, defeated, and humiliated. From 1918 through the 1930s, Germany suffered from hyperinflation, rampant unemployment, violence, instability, and attempts to overthrow the government. In 1933, the German people welcomed Adolf Hitler's appointment as chancellor, because he promised to deliver the nation from its political and economic crisis.

Could such a leader come to power again—and

would the world welcome him as the German people welcomed Hitler? Not only is such a thing possible, it's a biblical, prophetic certainty.

There's a tendency among certain ambitious men and women to seek positions of authoritarian power. The COVID-19 crisis revealed, even in the liberty-loving United States of America, that many government officials were all too eager to violate the First Amendment and take away our free exercise of religion. At first, church leaders were happy to cooperate with the government in trying to slow the transmission of the virus. Catholic and Protestant churches voluntarily suspended in-person worship services in early 2020.

But many officials responded by imposing harsh, arbitrary lockdowns on churches that made no scientific sense. The Catholic Diocese of Brooklyn was forced to petition the Supreme Court for protection from New York Governor Andrew Cuomo, who imposed limits of as few as ten worshippers per Mass.[1] In California, Governor Gavin Newsom sent a cease-and-desist letter to Pastor John MacArthur and Grace Community Church of Los Angeles, threatening jail time and a $1,000-per-day fine for defying the state's lockdown of churches. And Los Angeles Mayor Eric Garcetti threatened to cut off water and power to Grace Community Church while allowing certain businesses to remain open and permitting nightly downtown protests.[2]

Elected officials relished their "emergency" powers, ordering churches and businesses to shut down. They decided which activities were "essential" and which were "nonessential," arbitrarily depriving citizens of their livelihood and their religious liberty in the name of a "public health crisis." These officials often showed favoritism to political donors and cronies, making oppressive rules for everyone else while flouting those rules themselves. In response, Supreme Court Justice Samuel Alito said, "The pandemic has resulted in previously unimaginable restrictions on individual liberty."[3]

How will our leaders respond to the next pandemic? The next wave of protests and riots in the streets? The next earthquake or other natural disaster? When the next crisis comes, watch how quickly our leaders seek to take away our rights and control our lives. Watch how quickly they shut down the churches.

As Christians, we need to respect our leaders, to pray for them, and to obey the law. But we also have to hold our leaders accountable for respecting God's law and human liberty. We have to obey God rather than human beings. We must obey God even if it means respectfully defying the edicts of politicians.

THE CULMINATION OF HISTORY

The time is coming when the world will fall under the spell of the ultimate power-drunk ruler. The Bible calls this ruler the Antichrist. He will promise peace but deliver pain. The world will fear him. Followers of Jesus, however, must remember the Lord's words: "See to it that you are not alarmed" (Matt. 24:6). We need to live faithfully and boldly, knowing that the rise of the Antichrist could be just around the corner.

The culmination of history is approaching. The end of the world may be at hand. Yet Jesus tells us we should not be alarmed. Why? Because we are engraved in the palms of His hands. Because we are carried in His arms. Because we are the apple of His eye.

I believe that we Christians are indestructible—until God says otherwise. I am indestructible and so are you—until God says our life's work is complete.

God has promised in His Word: "If you say, 'The LORD is my refuge,' and you make the Most High your dwelling, no harm will overtake you, no disaster will come near your tent" (Ps. 91:9–10). And, "In peace I will lie down and sleep, for you alone, LORD, make me dwell in safety" (Ps. 4:8). And, "'No weapon forged against you will prevail, and you will refute every tongue that accuses you. This is the heritage of the servants of the LORD, and this is their vindication from me,' declares the LORD" (Isa. 54:17).

You see? These are God's promises. You are indestructible—until that time when your loving Father says, "It's time for you to come and live with Me forever."

As the world grows darker and more dangerous, we need to bulletproof ourselves and our families from the lies of "small-*a* antichrists"—false teachers and false preachers who would deceive us about salvation, judgment, heaven, and hell.

ANTICHRIST IN THE OLD TESTAMENT

The Bible speaks of the Antichrist in numerous passages, in both the Old and New Testaments. He was first identified in the prophetic Book of Daniel, chapter 7, which speaks of a king who will arise and vanquish three other powerful kings. This king "will speak against the Most High and oppress his holy people and try to change the set times and the laws." Later, he will be "completely destroyed forever" and "the sovereignty, power and greatness of all the kingdoms under heaven will be handed over to the holy people of the Most High. His kingdom will be an everlasting kingdom, and all rulers will worship and obey him" (vv. 25–27).

Daniel refers to the Antichrist again in chapter 11—"The king will do as he pleases. He will exalt and magnify himself above every god and will say unheard-of things against the God of gods. He will be successful until the time of wrath is completed, for what has been determined must take place" (v. 36).

In Daniel 12 we see a fascinating passage that speaks of the end-time as "a time of distress such as has not happened from the beginning of nations until then." At the end of that time of distress something wonderful happens: "But at that time your people—everyone whose name is found written in the book—will be delivered. Multitudes who sleep in the dust of the earth will awake: some to everlasting life, others to shame and everlasting contempt" (vv. 1–2). Though some people falsely claim that Old Testament Jews did not believe in the resurrection or eternal life, this is clearly an Old Testament promise of the resurrection of all believers, which will take place at the return of Jesus Christ.

The Daniel 12 prophecy goes on to affirm all who will live wisely and righteously for God and who spread the good news of salvation to others: "Those who are wise will shine like the brightness of the heavens, and those who lead many to righteousness, like the stars for ever and ever" (v. 3).

ANTICHRIST IN THE NEW TESTAMENT

In the Olivet Discourse, as we have seen, Jesus drew upon the Daniel prophecy to show that the fulfillment of the prediction of the Antichrist still lay in the future, shortly before the time of His return. Jesus may also make reference to the Antichrist in John's Gospel.

In John 14, Jesus speaks of His second coming, when He will take His followers to heaven: "My Father's house has many rooms; if that were not so, would I have told you that I am going there to prepare a place for you? And if I go and prepare a place for you, I will come back and take you to be with me that you also may be where I am" (vv. 2–3). Later in this same discussion, Jesus says, "I will not say much more to you, for *the prince of this world is coming*. He has no hold over me" (v. 30, emphasis added).

Who is "the prince of this world"? Some Bible

commentators say Jesus refers here to Satan, and that may be true. But the context of this discussion is that Jesus is going away, the Father will send the Holy Spirit to believers, and Jesus will later return to take the believers home to heaven. If "the prince of this world" is Satan, why would Jesus say that Satan is "coming"? Satan was already active in the world. I think the phrase "the prince of this world" may be a reference to the Antichrist, who would appear on the scene shortly before His second coming.

Jesus also seems to allude to the coming Antichrist when He says to the religious leaders who are persecuting Him, "I have come in my Father's name, and you do not accept me; but if someone else comes in his own name, you will accept him" (John 5:43). When the Antichrist arises, he will come in his own name—and many who have rejected Jesus will accept the Antichrist as their leader and even their god.

The word *Antichrist* appears in the Bible only four times, in the letters of 1 and 2 John (1 John 2:18, 2:22, 4:3, and 2 John 7). In 1 John 2:18, the apostle writes, "Dear children, this is the last hour; and as you have heard that the antichrist is coming, even now many antichrists have come. This is how we know it is the last hour." The phrase "as you have heard" makes it clear that the early church was well aware of prophecies of a future Antichrist. And the statement "even now many antichrists have come" makes it clear that the early church was plagued with false teachers, even as we are today.

John said, "This is how we know it is the last hour"— meaning, John and all the early believers were living as if Jesus could return at any moment. They were living just as Jesus told them to. They were waiting and watching, serving others and sharing the gospel, eagerly expecting Jesus to return at any moment. That is how we should live today, whether Jesus comes back today or a thousand years from now.

In 1 John 2:22, the apostle writes, "Who is the liar? It is whoever denies that Jesus is the Christ. Such a person is the antichrist—denying the Father and the Son." Here, the apostle John broadly defines "antichrist" as anyone who "denies that Jesus is the Christ" (that is, who denies that Jesus is the promised Messiah, the Savior of the world).

And in 1 John 4:3, John tells us that the refusal to acknowledge Jesus is "the spirit of antichrist"—and John tells us that "the spirit of antichrist" is both a future and present reality: "the spirit of the antichrist, which you have heard is coming and even now is already in the world."

Though the apostle Paul never uses the word "antichrist" in any of his letters, he spoke of the Antichrist in his major prophetic passage in 2 Thessalonians 2:1–12. There, he refuted the deceptive claims of false teachers who had arisen in the church. These lying teachers were claiming that Paul had announced that the Lord had already returned—and the church had been left behind. You can imagine how upset those believers were to hear this!

So Paul assured the believers that Jesus would not return until after the Antichrist—or, as Paul called him, "the man of lawlessness"—was revealed. He wrote:

> Don't let anyone deceive you in any way, for that day will not come until the rebellion occurs and the man of lawlessness is revealed, the man doomed to destruction. He will oppose and will exalt himself over everything that is called God or is worshiped, so that he sets himself up in God's temple, proclaiming himself to be God.
> —2 THESSALONIANS 2:3–4

Paul goes on to reassure the church that after the Antichrist is revealed, "the Lord Jesus will overthrow [him] with the breath of his mouth and destroy [him] by the splendor of his coming" (2 Thess. 2:8).

RECOGNIZING THE SPIRIT OF ANTICHRIST

In the Book of Revelation, John writes of his vision of the end-time. In Revelation 13, John gives us a detailed description of the Antichrist. John describes two beasts, one arising from the sea, the other from the land (vv. 1–18). The first beast represents the Antichrist, the final world ruler, who will be destroyed at the second coming of Christ. The second beast is probably a satanically inspired religious leader who supports the political reign of the first beast. Clearly both "beasts," both leaders, are possessed by the "spirit of antichrist," a spirit that denies that Jesus is the Messiah and Savior of the world.

The same John who wrote the Book of Revelation also told us that "even now many antichrists have come." Down through history, whenever a political figure, a religious figure, or a person of power and influence in society has denied that Jesus Christ is the Messiah, people have been quick to identify that person as the Antichrist. Ever since Satan was cast out of heaven for attempting to dethrone God, he has enlisted people in his opposition to God.

These "small-*a* antichrists" have always been numerous within and outside of the church, in every generation. The first century church was riddled with "small-*a* antichrists," and so is the twenty-first-century church. They do the bidding of Satan himself.

But there will come a point in history when *the* Antichrist with a capital A will be revealed. He will arise just before the return of Christ. He will literally take control of the entire planet, of all the nations on earth. He will arise at a time of great confusion and chaos in the world. He will arise during conditions of global fear and unrest. He will arise when the world is in political and financial upheaval.

Just as the entire world is desperate for order and security, one man will step forth with a message of hope and peace. Daniel 7:8 describes this leader as possessing "a mouth that spoke boastfully." I believe this describes a person who is a powerfully charismatic orator, who exudes a winsome charm, and who seems superhumanly brilliant. He will be everything people want a world leader to be. His speeches will strike a chord within the human heart. People will be drawn to him and he will unite the world under his rule.

For a time, he will deliver exactly what he has promised: Peace. Prosperity. Security. Hope. But once he has the world in his grip, he will remove the mask of the Messiah-like peacemaker—and reveal himself as a ruthless dictator. Above all, he will deny that Jesus is the only One worthy to be worshipped. Instead, he will demand that the world worships him.

A World Prepared for the Antichrist

Our world is already being prepared for the Antichrist. There are countless forces today that would normally oppose each other—yet they have joined forces in their opposition to Jesus Christ. They are united in their denial that Jesus is the only way of salvation.

Secular humanists and atheists have nothing at all in common with New Age mystics or Islamists. These groups would normally be at each others' throats. Secular humanists and atheists see New Agers as hopelessly irrational anti-intellectuals. And they see Islamists as dangerous religious fundamentalists who threaten the stability of society. Islamists, on the other hand, believe that anyone who doesn't worship Allah and honor Muhammad is an infidel.

Yet these opposing groups have one belief in common. They are all united in their total rejection of Jesus' claim to be the divine Son of God and the only way to God the Father.

Even the Christian world is not united about Jesus' claim to be the only way of salvation. A 2018 survey conducted by Ligonier Ministries and LifeWay Research found that many Americans who claim to hold "evangelical beliefs" have shockingly unbiblical notions about Jesus and salvation.

The Bible tells us, "There is no one righteous, not even one...for all have sinned and fall short of the glory of God" (Rom. 3:10, 23). Yet a majority of self-described "evangelicals"—52 percent—agree with the statement, "Most people are basically good."

Jesus said, "I am the way and the truth and the life. No one comes to the Father except through me" (John 14:6). And Peter declared, "Salvation is found in no one else, for there is no other name under heaven given to mankind by which we must be saved" (Acts 4:12). Yet a majority of self-described "evangelicals"—51 percent—agree with the statement, "God accepts the worship of all religions."

The Gospel of John declares, "In the beginning was the Word [i.e., Jesus, the Son of God], and the Word was with God, and the Word was God" (John 1:1). And Jesus Himself told the religious leaders who sought to stone Him and kill Him, "I and the Father are one" (John 10:30). In other words, Jesus claimed to be the eternal God, the Maker of the Universe, in human flesh. Yet a huge majority of self-described "evangelicals"—78 percent—agree with the statement, "Jesus was the first and greatest being created by God the Father."[4]

Could this survey be accurate? Do more than three-quarters of "evangelicals" believe that Jesus is a *created* being and not almighty God in human form?

WHAT DOES *EVANGELICAL* MEAN?

Part of the problem is that many people use the term *evangelical* so loosely that it has lost its meaning. I've heard people in the media use *evangelical* when referring to Christians in general, or Protestants, or even politically conservative Americans. But the word *evangelical* has a specific definition. An evangelical Christian is a person who believes in the doctrine of salvation by grace through faith in the atoning death and resurrection of Jesus, the Son of God.

Saying "I am an evangelical Christian" while believing that people are basically good, all religions lead to God, and Jesus is not God in human form is like saying "I'm a Green Bay Packers fan" while wearing a Chicago Bears jersey and rooting for the Packers' archrival.

The word *evangelical* stems from the Greek word *euangelion*, meaning gospel or good news. Rightly speaking, evangelicals are people who believe salvation and the forgiveness of sin come through Jesus alone. Authentic evangelicals believe in the authority of God's Word over every aspect of life. To claim to be an evangelical while denying that Jesus alone is the way to God and heaven is not merely a self-contradiction—it's heresy.

No wonder there is so much confusion in the church today. Clearly, there are many people in the pews—and, tragically, many in the pulpits—who espouse beliefs that come not from the Bible, but from the world.

Anyone who places tradition, personal opinion, or rationalism above the authority of God's Word is no evangelical.

Anyone who claims that humanity can be "saved" through social programs, political agendas, or progressive education is no evangelical.

Anyone who de-emphasizes the horror of sin and the need for the atoning cross of Christ is no evangelical.

Anyone who denies that God poured out His wrath on His crucified Son for the sake of lost humanity is no evangelical.

Anyone who calls the atonement of the crucifixion an act of "cosmic child abuse" by God the Father (as several self-styled "evangelicals" have said) is no evangelical.

Anyone who denies that people need to undergo a personal conversion by repentance and faith in order to receive eternal life is no evangelical.

A true evangelical is a true Christian. A false

"evangelical" is a false "Christian"—and Jesus and the letters of Paul, Peter, and John repeatedly warn that we should beware the false teachings of false "Christians." If you do not believe the foundational truths of the Bible, then no matter what you call yourself, you are not a true Christian.

If you are not a true Christian, then I urge you to repent and come to Him on His own terms and receive salvation.

DON'T BE DECEIVED

No one but God in heaven knows the day and hour the end-time will begin. But the apostle Paul tells us that the world is being prepared to welcome the Antichrist during the last act of the human drama:

> Don't let anyone deceive you in any way, for that day will not come until the rebellion occurs and the man of lawlessness is revealed, the man doomed to destruction. He will oppose and will exalt himself over everything that is called God or is worshiped, so that he sets himself up in God's temple, proclaiming himself to be God.
> —2 THESSALONIANS 2:3–4

When he appears, the Antichrist will offer a message that the masses are eager to hear—a message that people are basically good, that all religions lead to the same destination, that those who claim that Jesus is the only way to heaven are narrowminded dogmatists. The

Antichrist's message will be just what the masses want to hear. And he'll back up his claims with wonderful deeds. He will fix the broken economy, bring peace to troubled regions, and win the adoration of the masses.

Once he is firmly in power and crowds are worshipping him—he will turn, suddenly and viciously, on all the true believers in the Lord Jesus Christ. As Jesus said in Matthew 24:15, that is when you will see "standing in the holy place 'the abomination that causes desolation.'" As Paul said, he will set himself up in God's temple, proclaiming himself to be God. He will accompany these claims with fake "signs and wonders," fake "miracles," so that he will appear to possess superhuman power.

But where will he get all of his power? From Satan, of course. Satan is a spirit. To accomplish his goal, Satan needs a warm body—a human being—to be his spokesman. So the Antichrist will be possessed by Satan. He will do Satan's bidding, opposing God by denying Christ and persecuting true Christians.

Revelation 13:3 tells us, "One of the heads of the beast seemed to have had a fatal wound, but the fatal wound had been healed. The whole world was filled with wonder and followed the beast." This is a reference to the Antichrist and the false "miracles" he will perform.

Note the way John carefully words that statement: the Antichrist "*seemed* to have had a fatal wound." There was an *appearance* of a fatal wound; then that *apparent* wound was healed, as if by a miracle. This suggests that the Antichrist will fake his own death and resurrection, which will cause the whole world to be amazed. This "miracle" will cause people around the world to follow the Antichrist.

Notice that this satanic "miracle" of "death and resurrection" is a mockery of the true miracle of the death and resurrection of Jesus Christ. Everything the Antichrist does will be a counterfeit of the true works of Jesus Christ. The Antichrist will try to steal the glory that rightfully belongs to Jesus.

WILL THE CHURCH GO THROUGH THE TRIBULATION?

There are many wise, devoted scholars of the Bible who have varying views on the end-time and the return of Christ. Many of them are dear friends of mine.

Some say that Jesus will rapture His followers to heaven and while they are in heaven for seven years, all the horrors of the great tribulation will take place. (See Revelation 6–18.) Then, at the end of those seven years, Jesus will return to earth with His followers to reign for a thousand years (the Millennium Age).

Others say that we are in the Millennium Age right now. Still others say that the Millennium Age is a figure of speech.

I've studied all of these views, but I don't hold any of them. Though I respect the Bible scholars who espouse these views, I don't find them persuasive. I believe they interpret and systematize the Scriptures in a way that the Scriptures don't systematize themselves. Rather than take a hard and fast position on how the end-time will unfold, I prefer to hold fast to four biblical truths that are beyond dispute:

1. Only those who receive Jesus Christ as Lord and Savior will experience eternal life in heaven.

2. Jesus will return as He has repeatedly promised.

3. Jesus will judge all those who have rejected Him.

4. When Jesus appears, He will take all genuine believers to be with Him forever.

Those four truths are sufficient for me. I will trust in God, whether I go through the great tribulation or not. I will trust in God whether I see the Antichrist or I don't. It makes no difference to me.

When you and I trusted Jesus for our salvation, we also trusted Him with our eternal future. Many Christians speculate on what heaven will look like, based on glimpses we have in the New Testament. I don't need to speculate. All I know is that wherever Jesus is, that is heaven.

I sometimes wonder why we Christians cling so tenaciously to this life when we know that Jesus has a far more beautiful place prepared for all who love Him.

He has promised that, no matter what happens, He will never leave us nor forsake us. He has promised that neither death, nor life, nor angels, nor principalities, nor things present, nor things to come, nor powers, nor height, nor depth, nor any created thing will be able to separate us from the love of God that is in Christ Jesus our Lord (Rom. 8:38–39).

LOOK UP!

The Bible uses various images to depict the Antichrist—a beast, the man of lawlessness, and in Daniel, a horn, like the horn of the beast. Daniel describes the climactic moment of history in these words:

> As I watched, this horn [the Antichrist] was waging war against the holy people and defeating them, until the Ancient of Days came and pronounced judgment in favor of the holy people of the Most High, and the time came when they possessed the kingdom.
>
> —DANIEL 7:21–22

This is great news! Daniel tells us that, just as the Satan-possessed world leader seems invincible, just as his deceptive spell over the world seems unbreakable, the Lord Jesus—the Ancient of Days, the Messiah— will appear. He will smash the might of the Antichrist, destroy him, and lock up Satan forever.

All of history is building toward the moment Daniel describes in those two verses. This is the culmination of history, from Adam and Eve until that very moment. In the final analysis, this is all that matters.

The return of Jesus Christ will be sudden and tragic for those who are unprepared—but that day will *not* take believers by surprise. Those who are watching and waiting for the day of the Lord, those who are prepared to meet Him at any time, will rejoice at that moment.

Among those who will be unprepared and devastated on that day will be many who denied the existence of God, many who followed false religions, many who mocked and persecuted the church. But there will also be many who call themselves "Christians" who will be devastated on that day, because they had denied the divinity of Christ, they had denied the claims of Christ, they had denied the resurrection and the authority of Christ, and they had departed from biblical faith.

Faithful believers will not be shaken during the great tribulation. A faithful believer who sees the rise of the Antichrist will compare world events with the prophecies of Jesus, Daniel, Peter, Paul, and John—and that faithful believer will say, "Jesus is coming soon! I'm ready, Lord!" A faithful believer will be thrilled and filled with expectation and hope.

When you see church leaders weaken and water down the gospel for the sake of being popular and accepted by the world, don't be shaken. Hold fast to your faith in the Lord Jesus Christ. Cast out any idols that hold you back from an absolute commitment to Jesus. Continue serving diligently in His name. Continue sharing the

gospel with everyone around you. Continue living joyfully for Jesus.

When this world seems to be at its darkest, look up!
The day is drawing near. As the apostle Paul wrote:

> And now you know what is holding him back,
> so that he may be revealed at the proper time.
> For the secret power of lawlessness is already at
> work; but the one who now holds it back will
> continue to do so till he is taken out of the way.
> And then the lawless one will be revealed, whom
> the Lord Jesus will overthrow with the breath
> of his mouth and destroy by the splendor of his
> coming.
> —2 Thessalonians 2:6–8

As the restraining power of the Holy Spirit is being
withdrawn from the earth, when it seems that all hell
is breaking loose and Satan has assumed total control—
look up! The revelation of the Antichrist may seem
like the end of the world—but his destruction is just
around the corner. Soon, the Lord Jesus will overthrow
the Antichrist and destroy Satan.

Don't Gamble With Eternity

Oprah Winfrey overcame many obstacles to become
a world-famous talk show host and actress. Her show,
The Oprah Winfrey Show, became the highest-rated
television program of its kind during its twenty-five-
year run. She introduced many authors and their

books to her television audience, and it was said that Oprah's word of approval on a book was worth a million copies sold.

Many of the authors she hosted were promoting false gospels and New Age "spirituality," including Gary Zukav, Eckhart Tolle, and Marianne Williamson. Oprah also introduced her audience to the pseudo-spiritual self-help program, "The Secret," which claimed that positive emotional states could enable a person to shape the future by attracting "positive vibrations."

On one occasion, Oprah told her audience, "God is a feeling experience and not a believing experience. If your religion is a believing experience...then that's not truly God."[5]

On another occasion, she asked her audience, "How can there be only one way to heaven or to God?" A woman in the audience responded, "What about Jesus?" In a defiant tone, Oprah threw the question back at the woman, saying, "What about Jesus?...There couldn't possibly be [only] one way."[6]

A dear Christian friend told me about a conversation she had with one of her friends, a churchgoer and a devoted Oprah fan: "I told her that she needed to be very discerning about the false religions that were promoted by many of Oprah's guests. When I said that, she became offended and enraged. She told me I was close-minded against other forms of spirituality. Our friendship was damaged because I warned her against false teachers."

There is often a price to pay for holding fast to the truth of God's Word. It may cost you some friends. It may put barriers between you and people you care about. People often become very angry when defending false beliefs. But if you care about them, you must take the risk and speak the truth. You must warn people about the spirit of "small-*a* antichrist" that is all around us. You must tell people that Jesus *is* the only way to heaven, the only way to God the Father.

Of course, I'm not saying that Oprah Winfrey is the Antichrist. But anyone who denies that Jesus is the only way to God the Father is calling Jesus a liar—and is expressing the spirit of antichrist.

When the Antichrist appears, he will place the world under such a spell that his followers will begin persecuting Christians in his name. It will get vicious and violent. They will not put up with Christians saying that Jesus is the only way to God. They will claim that Christians are bigoted and intolerant of other religions— even though their intolerance toward Christianity will be through the roof.

I won't sugarcoat the truth. I will tell you plainly that being a Christian in the end-time will be incredibly difficult. It will mean being hated and persecuted for your faith.

But I guarantee that even if you are hunted down, abused, and killed for your faith in Jesus, it will have been worth it. You will have eternal life with Jesus in heaven. When He returns, you will be full of joy at

His appearing while the unsaved world despairs. Only Jesus offers true security in a collapsing world.

Most important of all, you will have the honor and privilege of being a partner with God in the final destruction of Satan. As the apostle Paul wrote in Romans 16:20, "The God of peace will soon crush Satan under your feet. The grace of our Lord Jesus be with you." Imagine, God has promised to crush Satan *under our feet*! What a thrill it will be to take part in the annihilation of our ancient enemy.

If you have never received Jesus as your Lord and Savior, I must ask you one last time before you close this book: Do you *really* want to gamble with your eternal soul? Or do you want to settle your eternal destiny here and now?

Come to the only One who can save, the One who died to deliver you from death to life. He will give you His peace and joy. No matter what the future holds, you will be secure forever in His hands.

APPENDIX

Recently, Stephen Strang, founder and CEO of Charisma Media, interviewed Michael Youssef about the invasion of Ukraine by the Russians. Pertinent to this book, their conversation sheds light on this devastating situation from a spiritual perspective, emphasizing that ultimately Jesus is victorious. The interview is included here for further information.

Steve Strang: Why don't we start by you telling me what you feel is the significance of this invasion from a spiritual point of view.

Michael Youssef: Here's what I've found out just as early as this morning: The godly Russian believers who love the Lord Jesus, and there are godly Ukrainians who love the Lord Jesus, are packing the churches. They are crying to God, and they're praying, and they're praying for each other. You see, this is not nation warring against nation. This is one dictator who's imposing his will on another nation. Putin has been telegraphing this for months. And the sad part about this is what Ronald Reagan warned us about—weakness invites war. Now we are seeing this. The weaker America becomes, the more wars are going to happen. This is just the beginning. We are going to see China doing some mischief in Taiwan. Iran is going to be doing some mischief. All because they have tested the will of the United States and found it wanting.

Strang: Well, that's an interesting observation. I have had the privilege of being in both countries. In fact, I have been in what was the former Soviet Union five times. And in the Ukraine, three times. All of it back in the 1990s, but I know a lot has changed since then. I was visiting Christians and went to a lot of churches. Just interesting to be there.

As communism was collapsing, I remembered being in the churches and the men sat on one side and the women on the other, which is odd to us Americans. There are some great churches there. As I recall, they were on fire for God, and they actually had more freedom than I expected. These are sincere God-loving people. But they were also concerned about having freedom from communism. I remember that the Ukrainians I was around talked about how they resented having to speak Russian, resented being a part of the Soviet Union. As far as they were concerned, it was a separate country, like some of the others including Latvia, Lithuania, and Hungary. But now the United Nations is saying they never really registered their borders. And so it's not really a country.

What do you think about all that? Or do you even know the answer?

Youssef: I have an answer. You don't live as long as I have without having an answer. This is globalism. The United Nations has been leading the world toward this one-world government globalism. The more these actors with a BA in Russia or in China or in other languages are leading things, the worse it will get. The United Nation bureaucrats are happy to see this. We are seeing a great reset. Even with a major corporation like BlackRock, they are literally bullying other corporations if they are not woke and if they are not globalist, and if they are not one-world order. You know, they don't get the business. We are seeing this is just part of the varied forces that have been working for a long time to create this one-world order. I have been saying this for a number of years. I honestly believe that Satan is preparing the world for the Antichrist.

In the past, people jumped the gun and said Hitler's the Antichrist or Mussolini's the Antichrist. This one's the Antichrist, and that one is the Antichrist. My old friend the late John Haggai used to say there were more Christians embarrassed when Hitler died than there were Germans. This is the problem: we must not jump the gun. We are to go to Matthew 24 to find out what

Jesus said. Jesus makes it very clear for the outside world; these things are going to come as a surprise—even His return is going to be like a thief in the night.

For the believers, it is like a childbirth. Elizabeth and I have four children and eleven grandchildren. And you know, the intervals between labor pains when they get closer and closer, the baby is about to be born. And that's what Jesus said in Matthew 24. Wars and rumors of wars, earthquakes, all these things have been with us for a long time. But when you see them coming on fast intervals, you know that the baby is about to be born.

So those of us who are looking up, the apostle Paul said, there is a special crown for those who love his appearing. We realize that these things are not by happenstance, they're not accidents. They are things serving God's purpose ultimately. And of course, Satan is trying to get in the middle. He knows this "day of appearing" is getting near, so he's intensifying his persecution of Christians.

Brother Stephen, when I see this so-called deconstruction—where megachurch pastors and Christian singers are turning their back on Christ, saying: "We are no longer Christians; we don't believe what we preached"—it is heartbreaking. Or, after years of church life...some are essentially watering it down so much it's really unrecognizable. When you see all of that, and then we also see thousands upon thousands of people in the Middle East and North Africa coming to

Christ, and when they come to Christ, they're literally signing their death warrant, yet they do it with joy— this convinces me that the Lord is beginning to gather His sheep together. He has elected separating the sheep from the goats. This is very exciting for Christians.

When we see these things, we need to be praying for the believers in Ukraine and in Russia, and in the Middle East, and in China, and elsewhere. Because you know, we are one church. We will be together in heaven for all of eternity from every language type, tribe, and nation. As Christians, we need the Church of Jesus Christ in America to keep praying for the church worldwide.

Strang: Very well said. I want to talk to you about prayer. But let's go back to what you said earlier about the Antichrist. The spirit of antichrist has been here since the early church. The Scriptures speak of the spirit of Antichrist, yet the Scriptures seem to say that there will become a powerful leader that the Bible calls the Antichrist. He will be a person who calls for peace.

I just want your opinion about this. There are those who say that Putin is trying to position himself as the most powerful leader in the world. Yes, because he of course, he sees leaders like Biden and Trudeau and Macron as anything but strong, right?

Putin knows what to say; he's a strong man. But because there's a vacuum, don't we believe that a leader is going to arise? He is going to say peace, peace, and everyone's gonna say, finally, someone is bringing us peace? And that is really the beginning of where all of this is going. Could this just be the thing that triggers that? Or is this just one more war and rumor of war that the Bible predicted?

Youssef: Well, of course, we don't know. I mean, we really don't know.

But personally I think that from the descriptions that we see in the Scripture, especially Daniel and Revelation, there is going to be a charming guy where everyone says, "Wow." But Putin doesn't have that charisma. I am not saying he is or he is not the one, but I really think that the world has to know for sure. The world is moving toward that person. When chaos is everywhere, he is going to arise.

Everyone, whether it be folks in Israel, in the Middle East, North America, Russia, or China, they're going to say, "Wow, finally, we have a truly charming person." He's going to be so charming that he is going to be winning the world by devotion. And people of every nation will literally be saying, "He is the one who's going to be our savior." Now, whether all of these events are going to give rise to him or not is yet to come. Nobody really knows. The Lord Jesus said, "Nobody knows; but when we see him, we will know."

As you know, the church is divided. Some people think, "We'll be out of here before that happens." Some others say, "We're going to be here for the tribulation." Still others think we have time, three and a half years—a middle tribulation rescue. I've never really gotten bogged down in all of the speculation.

I know one thing for sure: the Scriptures say that there is going to be a global move. And that global move will be worshipping one person who is a front for Satan, who will be empowered by Satan to perform supernatural miracles. Don't forget that he is going to have power to perform supernatural miracles. Literally, the world will be bowing to him voluntarily, not by force.

So whether all of current events in our world are giving rise to him, we are going to find out soon. But when we do see him, we will know it. The believers will know it, and they will say, "He is the one." That's if my friends who say we're going to be here are right. But if my friends who say we're going to be out of here before all this [happens—if they are right—then I'm ready to go]. I am a chicken like the rest of them; I would rather go to heaven before the tribulation.

Strang: We know that the Bible says, "All things work together for good." No matter how bad things get—and things look pretty bad in Ukraine right now. People will be listening to this much later when a lot of other things have happened. The peacekeeping forces moved into the cities less than twenty-four hours ago. But yet there's so much fear.

Gold prices have gone crazy. The stock market is rocky. People are afraid. So, what would you say to people who are afraid of these wars? How is it going to disrupt the world economy? Is it going to draw in other major powers? Look at World War I. There was an unfortunate assassination in a minor country, and then all the other countries got involved. We had a World War. What would you say to people who are afraid? And how would you tell people, Jesus followers, how to pray?

Youssef: This is a great, great question. It really is.

We should never be afraid of whatever happens. Fear is the instrument of the enemy. It is the Bible that calls fear what it is—it is a spirit from Satan. He has no right or any hold upon Christians. And we need to fight fear with every ounce of spiritual energy. But at the same time, when we think of Revelation 18, and even World War I or World War II, they were not as globally connected as they are now. So in Revelation, it says all of the merchants of the world. John is talking about the globe, a globe that is so interconnected. Right now, there is moaning and weeping. There is going to be a collapse, a financial collapse. I tell people all the time, if you are dependent on Wall Street for your prosperity, if you are dependent on the Dow-Jones Industrial Average for your prosperity, then you're in trouble. But if you are depending on God, and He's your provider, and you've been faithful with God, you have nothing to fear. The psalmist said, "I have been young, now I'm old, I have never seen the righteous forsaken, nor his children begging for bread. So this is a time not to fear, but to lift up our heads because the day of our redemption is drawing nigh."

Strang: Amen. And as we wrap up this interview, I want you to tell people specifically how we can pray. You know, the Bible talks about prayers of agreement. We are in a real spirit war, which is much bigger than the physical wars that are going on. So how should we pray?

Youssef: Absolutely. My privilege.

First of all, we need to pray for the believers worldwide. We need to specifically now because it is in the news. We need to be praying for the believers in Russia, who are in trouble as soon as they criticize Putin. We need to pray for the believers in Ukraine. Even though they have some freedom, they are still crying out to God. We need to pray for believers in every corner of China. The churches are closing down. The people have been tortured. And in Pakistan, [Christians have been slandered, accused of blasphemy against Allah and Muhammad, and one man was stoned to death by an enraged mob].

We need to be praying for the persecuted church. Persecution has been going on. In fact, there are more martyrs who died for Christ during the twentieth century than the first century—in fact, the first three centuries combined. And so we need to be praying for the church worldwide, because that is the body of Christ.

These are the brothers and sisters with whom we are going to spend eternity.

That's the first thing we need to do. Then we need to pray for an awakening. An awakening so that the lost can come to know Jesus Christ and look to Him as Savior and Lord. Believe in Him and place faith in Him, especially in these times when people are fearing. They will see a believer, not fearing at all, living in peace and real joy. They will say, "Why is that? We need our lives to be a witness for Christ to the world."

Strang: Will you pray for us?

Youssef: I'll be honored to pray right now: "Father, I thank You for my brother, Steve Strang. Lord, I pray in the name of Jesus that everyone reading this right now, wherever they may be in the world, that they will be encouraged to know that Jesus is victorious. We have read the last chapter, and it says that we win.

"Father, I pray that You would give us a spirit of victory, not a victimhood, that You would lift up the eyes of Your children to heaven, to know that this is their home, that they're heading home, that our citizenship is in heaven. We love living in this great country of the United States of America. And I'm very grateful as an immigrant to be here.

"Lord, remind us, remind us again and again that we are on our way to heaven. We are sojourners, and help us to take as many people to heaven with us as You can allow us through the grace and the mercy and the sovereignty of God. I pray all of this in the name of Jesus and through the power of His blood and in the strength of the Holy Spirit. Amen and amen."

Strang: And amen.

It's not very often that journalistic interviews end in prayer, but they probably should. Thank you, Dr. Youssef, for taking time during this very historic period. It is a blessing to pray with you and an opportunity we can all take seriously. God bless you.

NOTES

Chapter 1

1. Tom Engelhardt, "The End of the World Is Closer Than It Seems," *The Nation*, July 2, 2021, https://www.thenation.com/article/world/nuclear-apocolypse/.

2. Janet Daley, "Scared Out of Their Wits by the Covid Paranoia, Britons Long to Repent, Submit and Be Controlled," *The Telegraph*, July 24, 2021, https://www.telegraph.co.uk/news/2021/07/24/scared-wits-covid-paranoia-britons-long-repent-submit-controlled/.

3. Milutin Gjaja and Laura Gersony, "Is This the End of the World?," *Chicago Maroon*, February 1, 2021, https://www.chicagomaroon.com/article/2021/2/1/end-world/; "The Doomsday Clock, Explained," *UChicago News*, accessed April 26, 2022, https://news.uchicago.edu/explainer/what-is-the-doomsday-clock#:~:text=When%20it%20was%20created%20in,in%20its%20hand%2Dsetting%20deliberations; John Mecklin, ed., "At Doom's Doorstep: It Is 100 Seconds to Midnight—2022 Doomsday Clock Statement," *Bulletin of the Atomic Scientists*, January 20, 2022, https://thebulletin.org/doomsday-clock/current-time/.

4. Abraham Mahshie, "Russia Invades Ukraine, Biden Calls on NATO for 'Strong, United'

193

Response," *Air Force Magazine*, February 24, 2022, https://www.airforcemag.com/russia-attacks-ukraine-biden-calls-on-nato-for-strong-united-response/.

5. Julian Vierlinger, "UN: Ukraine Refugee Crisis Is Europe's Biggest Since WWII," Atlantic Council, April 20, 2022, https://www.atlanticcouncil.org/blogs/ukrainealert/un-ukraine-refugee-crisis-is-europes-biggest-since-wwii/; Jennifer Hassan and Sammy Westfall, "Ukraine War Pushes Global Displaced to Record High, U.N. Says," *Washington Post*, June 16, 2022, https://www.washingtonpost.com/world/2022/06/16/refugee-displaced-ukraine-syria-afghanistan/.

6. Laurel Wamsley, "Rape Has Reportedly Become a Weapon in Ukraine. Finding Justice May Be Difficult," NPR, April 30, 2022, https://www.npr.org/2022/04/30/1093339262/ukraine-russia-rape-war-crimes; Robert Greenall, "Ukraine War: Refugee From Popasna Spots Looted Possessions on Russian Tank," BBC News, May 31, 2022, https://www.bbc.com/news/world-europe-61643533; Lee Brown, "Around 300 Ukrainians Were Killed in Bombing of Mariupol Theater Marked 'Children': Council," *New York Post*, March 25, 2022, https://nypost.com/2022/03/25/around-300-killed-in-bombing-of-mariupol-theater-marked-children-council/.

7. Vanessa Romo, "A Ukrainian Mom Scribbled Her Contact Info on Her Daughter's Back as the War Erupted," NPR, April 8, 2022, https://www.npr.org/2022/04/08/1091542359/ukrainian-mom-daughter-writing-back-instagram-war-makoviy.

8. Fiona Harvey, "Coronavirus Pandemic 'Will Cause Famine of Biblical Proportions': Governments Must Act Now to Stop 265 Million Starving, Warns World Food Programme Boss," *The Guardian*, April 21, 2020, https://www.theguardian.com/global-development/2020/apr/21/coronavirus-pandemic-will-cause-famine-of-biblical-proportions.

9. "Fact Sheet: United States Bans Imports of Russian Oil, Liquefied Natural Gas, and Coal," The White House, March 8, 2022, https://www.whitehouse.gov/briefing-room/statements-releases/2022/03/08/fact-sheet-united-states-bans-imports-of-russian-oil-liquefied-natural-gas-and-coal/; Declan Walsh and Valerie Hopkins, "Russia Seeks Buyers for Plundered Ukraine Grain, U.S. Warns," *New York Times*, updated June 8, 2022, https://www.nytimes.com/2022/06/05/world/africa/ukraine-grain-russia-sales.html; Dea Bankova, Prasanta Kumar Dutta, and Michael Ovaska, "The War in Ukraine Is Fuelling a Global Food Crisis," Reuters, May 30, 2022,

https://graphics.reuters.com/UKRAINE-CRISIS/ FOOD/zjvqkgomjvx/; Lauren Gambino, "US Bans Import of Russian Vodka, Seafood and Diamonds," *The Guardian*, March 11, 2022, https://www.theguardian.com/world/2022/ mar/11/us-bans-russian-vodka-seafood- diamonds-ukraine; Francesco Guarascio, "EU Slashes 10% of Russian Imports With New Sweeping Sanctions," Reuters, April 8, 2022, https://www.reuters.com/world/europe/ eu-adopts-new-sanctions-against-russia- including-coal-import-ban-2022-04-08/.

10. Stephanie Hegarty, "How Can Ukraine Export Its Harvest to the World?," BBC News, May 26, 2022, https://www.bbc.com/news/world- europe-61583492.

11. Tom Polansek and Ana Mano, "As Sanctions Bite Russia, Fertilizer Shortage Imperils World Food Supply," Reuters, March 23, 2022, https:// www.reuters.com/business/sanctions-bite- russia-fertilizer-shortage-imperils-world-food- supply-2022-03-23/; Editor OilPrice.com, "The Threat of a Global Food Crisis Is Growing," Yahoo! Finance, March 28, 2022, https://nz.finance. yahoo.com/news/threat-global-food-crisis- growing-193000653.html.

12. Jack Nicas, "Ukraine War Threatens to Cause a Global Food Crisis," *New York Times*, March 20, 2022, https://www.nytimes.com/2022/03/20/world/ americas/ukraine-war-global-food-crisis.html.

13. Keith Good, "'It's Going to Be Real,' President Biden on War-Related Food Shortages," Illinois Farm Policy News, March 25, 2022, https://farmpolicynews.illinois.edu/2022/03/its-going-to-be-real-president-biden-on-war-related-food-shortages/.

14. Alex Domash and Lawrence H. Summers, "Overheating Conditions Indicate High Probability of a US Recession," VoxEU, April 13, 2022, https://voxeu.org/article/overheating-conditions-indicate-high-probability-us-recession.

15. Eric Boehm, "COVID Stimulus Checks Worsened Inflation," *Reason*, April 8, 2022, https://reason.com/2022/04/08/covid-stimulus-checks-worsened-inflation/.

16. Jacqui Heinrich and Adam Sabes, "Gen. Milley Says Kyiv Could Fall Within Seventy-Two Hours if Russia Decides to Invade Ukraine: Sources," Fox News, February 5, 2022, https://www.foxnews.com/us/gen-milley-says-kyiv-could-fall-within-72-hours-if-russia-decides-to-invade-ukraine-sources.

17. Jack Dutton, "How Many Tanks Has Russia Lost in Ukraine?," *Newsweek*, March 11, 2022, https://www.newsweek.com/how-many-tanks-has-russia-lost-ukraine-1687207.

18. Eleanor Watson, "Top U.S. Military Officer Expects Ukraine Conflict to Be 'Measured in Years,'" CBS News, April 5, 2022, https://www.cbsnews.com/news/ukraine-conflict-years-mark-milley-house-armed-services-committee/.

19. Ian Bremmer, "How Does the War in Ukraine End?," April 3, 2022, in *Making Sense*, podcast, https://www.samharris.org/podcasts/making-sense-episodes/277-how-does-the-war-in-ukraine-end, transcribed by the author.

20. Derek Lowe, "Gain of Function," *Science*, October 26, 2021, https://www.science.org/content/blog-post/gain-function.

21. "Life After Default," The White House, October 6, 2021, https://www.whitehouse.gov/cea/written-materials/2021/10/06/life-after-default/.

22. Ernest Hemingway, *The Sun Also Rises* (New York: Oxford University Press, 2002), 115.

Chapter 2

1. "Baker in Spotlight After Court Win in Gay Wedding Cake Case," Associated Press, June 4, 2018, https://apnews.com/article/130137ace2e84 16aa207456827fae92b; Matt Lavietes, "Christian Florist Settles After Refusing Service for a Same-Sex Wedding," NBC News, November 18, 2021, https://www.nbcnews.com/nbc-out/out-news/christian-florist-settles-refusing-service-sex-wedding-rcna6065; Zack Smith, "Little Sisters of Poor Win Big at Supreme Court, but Fight Isn't Over," Heritage Foundation, July 9, 2020, https://www.heritage.org/religious-liberty/commentary/little-sisters-poor-win-big-supreme-court-fight-isnt-over.

2. Jon Brown, "Pastor Andrew Brunson 'Astounded at the Speed With Which the US Is Imploding' and Predicts Persecution," *Washington Examiner,* July 15, 2019, https://www.washingtonexaminer.com/news/pastor-andrew-brunson-astounded-at-the-speed-with-which-the-us-is-imploding-and-predicts-persecution.

3. "Titus' Siege of Jerusalem," Livius.org, October 10, 2020, https://www.livius.org/articles/concept/roman-jewish-wars/roman-jewish-wars-4/.

4. Harry Thomas Frank, *An Archaeological Companion to the Bible* (London: SCM Press, 1972), 249.

5. "COVID-19 Projections," Institute for Health Metrics and Evaluation, November 17, 2021, https://covid19.healthdata.org/global?view=cumulative-deaths&tab=trend.

6. Will Stone and Carrie Feibel, "The U.S. 'Battles' Coronavirus, but Is It Fair to Compare Pandemic to a War?," NPR, February 3, 2021, https://www.npr.org/sections/health-shots/2021/02/03/962811921/the-u-s-battles-coronavirus-but-is-it-fair-to-compare-pandemic-to-a-war.

7. "Top 10 Largest Armies in the World 2021," Infos-10, September 14, 2021, https://infos10.com/largest-army-in-the-world/; GFP, "2021 China Military Strength," Global Fire Power, 2021, https://www.globalfirepower.com/

country-military-strength-detail.php?country_
id=china.

8. Michael M. Phillips, "China Seeks First
Military Base on Africa's Atlantic Coast,
U.S. Intelligence Finds," *Wall Street Journal*,
December 5, 2021, https://www.wsj.com/articles/
china-seeks-first-military-base-on-africas-
atlantic-coast-u-s-intelligence-finds-11638726327.

9. Ashish Dangwal, "China on Verge of Gobbling
Entebbe Airport Where Israel Once Conducted
One of World's Most Daring Military Ops,"
EurAsian Times, November 30, 2021, https://
eurasiantimes.com/china-gobbling-entebbe-
airport-israel-orlds-most-daring-military-ops/.

10. Brahma Chellaney, "China's Debt-Trap Diplomacy,"
The Hill, May 2, 2021, https://thehill.com/opinion/
international/551337-chinas-debt-trap-diplomacy.

11. Jarrett Stepman, "China Wants You to Be a
Woke 'Anti-Racist' While It Pursues Ethnic
Cleansing," *Daily Signal*, August 20, 2021, https://
www.dailysignal.com/2021/08/20/china-wants-
you-to-be-a-woke-anti-racist-while-they-pursue-
ethnic-cleansing/; Miles Maochun Yu, "Beijing's
Woke Propaganda War in America," Hoover
Institution, May 5, 2021, https://www.hoover.org/
research/beijings-woke-propaganda-war-america;
Matt Pottinger, "Beijing's American Hustle: How
Chinese Grand Strategy Exploits U.S. Power,"
Foreign Affairs, September/October 2021, https://
www.foreignaffairs.com/articles/asia/2021-08-23/

beijings-american-hustle; "China Hides Identities
of Top Scientific Recruits Amidst Growing US
Scrutiny," Nature, updated October 26, 2018,
https://www.nature.com/articles/d41586-018-
07167-6.

12. Carrie Gracie, "The Thoughts of Chairman Xi,"
BBC News, October 13, 2017, https://www.bbc.
co.uk/news/resources/idt-sh/Thoughts_Chairman_
Xi.

13. Maura Moynihan, "Disney's China Problem:
West's Elite Covering up CCP's Misdeeds," *Asian
Age*, October 21, 2020, https://www.asianage.com/
opinion/columnists/211020/maura-moynihan-
disneys-china-problem-wests-elite-covering-up-
ccps-misdeeds.html.

14. Ben Pickman, "Enes Kanter Calls Out Nike,
Co-Founder Phil Knight Over Forced Labor
in China," *Sports Illustrated*, October 26, 2021,
https://www.si.com/nba/2021/10/26/enes-kanter-
protest-nike-china-injustices; Warner Todd Huston,
"Nike Exec Assures China: 'Nike Is a Brand That
Is of China and for China,'" Breitbart, June 25,
2021, https://www.breitbart.com/sports/2021/06/25/
nike-exec-assures-china-nike-is-a-brand-that-is-of-
china-and-for-china/.

15. Ben Church, "Enes Kanter Says Nike Is 'Scared to
Speak Up' Against China and Wears 'Modern Day
Slavery' Shoes in Protest of Uyghur Treatment,"
CNN, October 26, 2021, https://www.cnn.

com/2021/10/26/football/enes-kanter-nike-china-protest-spt-intl/index.html.

16. Jack Nicas, Raymond Zhong, and Daisuke Wakabayashi, "Censorship, Surveillance and Profits: A Hard Bargain for Apple in China," *New York Times*, updated June 17, 2021, https://www.nytimes.com/2021/05/17/technology/apple-china-censorship-data.html.

17. Dave Gibson, "Was That New iPhone Made With Chinese Slave Labor?," US Incorporated, March 16, 2020, https://usinc.org/was-that-new-iphone-made-with-chinese-slave-labor/.

18. Nick Schifrin and Dan Sagalyn, "Nuclear Weapons, Taiwan and Other Key Issues Addressed on Biden-Xi Call," PBS, November 16, 2021, https://www.pbs.org/newshour/show/nuclear-weapons-taiwan-and-other-key-issues-addressed-on-biden-xi-call.

19. Chris Smith, "Opinion: The World Must Stand Against China's War on Religion," *Washington Post*, December 27, 2018, https://www.washingtonpost.com/opinions/the-world-must-stand-against-chinas-war-on-religion/2018/12/27/115685aa-0a0f-11e9-85b6-41c0fe0c5b8f_story.html; Nina Shea and Bob Fu, "Inside China's War on Christians," *Wall Street Journal*, May 30, 2019, https://www.wsj.com/articles/inside-chinas-war-on-christians-11559256446.

Chapter 3

1. Economist Staff, "What Is the Economic Cost of Covid-19?," *The Economist*, January 7, 2021, https://www.economist.com/finance-and-economics/2021/01/09/what-is-the-economic-cost-of-covid-19.

2. Gideon Lichfield, "We're Not Going Back to Normal," *MIT Technology Review*, March 17, 2020, https://www.technologyreview.com/2020/03/17/905264/coronavirus-pandemic-social-distancing-18-months/.

3. Sir Isaac Newton, *Observations Upon the Prophecies of Daniel and the Apocalypse of St. John*, quoted in *An Introduction to the Critical Study and Knowledge of the Holy Scriptures*, vol. 4, edited by Thomas Hartwell Horne (London: Longmans, Green, and Co., 1877), 632.

4. Tom Phillips, "Xi Jinping: Does China Truly Love 'Big Daddy Xi'—or Fear Him?," *The Guardian*, September 19, 2015, https://www.theguardian.com/world/2015/sep/19/xi-jinping-does-china-truly-love-big-daddy-xi-or-fear-him.

5. Nectar Gan, "Replace Pictures of Jesus with Xi to Escape Poverty, Chinese Villagers Urged," *South China Morning Post*, November 14, 2017, https://www.scmp.com/news/china/policies-politics/article/2119699/praise-xi-jinping-not-jesus-escape-poverty-christian; Simon Denyer, "Jesus Won't Save You—President Xi Jinping Will, Chinese Christians Told,"

Washington Post, November 14, 2017, https://www.washingtonpost.com/news/worldviews/wp/2017/11/14/jesus-wont-save-you-president-xi-jinping-will-chinese-christians-told/.

6. Arielle Del Turco, "China to Christians: We're Rewriting the Bible, and You'll Use It or Else," Family Research Council, October 9, 2021, https://www.frc.org/op-eds/china-to-christians-were-rewriting-the-bible-and-youll-use-it-or-else.

7. "1 Samuel 19—The Eye of the Tiger," Calvary Chapel, September 15, 2013, https://www.calvarychapeloflafayette.org/teachings/1-samuel-19-the-eye-of-the-tiger/.

Chapter 4

1. Robert Browning, *Poetical Works* (London: Smith Elder and Co., 1897), 202.

2. Paul Rincon, "Nasa Dart Asteroid Spacecraft: Mission to Smash Into Dimorphos Space Rock Launches," BBC News, November 24, 2021, https://www.bbc.com/news/science-environment-59327293; Joey Roulette, "NASA Just Launched a Spacecraft That Will Crash Into an Asteroid," *New York Times*, November 24, 2021, https://www.nytimes.com/2021/11/23/science/nasa-dart-launch-asteroid.html.

3. Cassidy Ward, "The Asteroid Apophis Isn't Likely to Hit Earth. But if It Did, What Could We Do?," SYFY, November 13, 2020, https://

www.syfy.com/syfy-wire/asteroid-impact-apophis-hit-earth-science.

4. Billy Graham, "J. Edwin Orr," J. Edwin Orr, accessed July 18, 2022, https://jedwinorr.com/about-j-edwin-orr/.

5. J. Edwin Orr, "Prayer and Revival," J. Edwin Orr, October 17, 2018, http://jedwinorr.com/resources/articles/prayandrevival.pdf.

6. Orr, "Prayer and Revival."

7. Orr, "Prayer and Revival."

8. Orr, "Prayer and Revival."

Chapter 5

1. "How Has World Population Growth Changed Over Time?," Our World in Data, accessed April 22, 2022, https://ourworldindata.org/world-population-growth#how-has-world-population-growth-changed-over-time; "Historical Estimates of World Population," US Census Bureau, October 8, 2021, https://www.census.gov/data/tables/time-series/demo/international-programs/historical-est-worldpop.html.

2. James Belgrave and Peyvand Khorsandi, "Acute Hunger at Five-Year High, Study Warns, as Famine Looms for Millions," World Food Programme, May 5, 2021, https://www.wfp.org/news/acute-food-insecurity-soars-five-year-high-warns-global-report-food-crises.

3. David Russell Schilling, "Knowledge Doubling Every 12 Months, Soon to Be Every 12 Hours,"

Industry Tap, April 19, 2013, https://www.
industrytap.com/knowledge-doubling-every-12-
months-soon-to-be-every-12-hours/3950.

4. Daniel Engber and Adam Federman, "The
Lab-Leak Debate Just Got Even Messier,"
The Atlantic, September 24, 2021, updated
September 26, 2021, https://www.theatlantic.
com/science/archive/2021/09/lab-leak-pandemic-
origins-even-messier/620209/.

5. Abené Clayton, "'Walgreens Fed My Family':
Inside the San Francisco Stores Closing Over
'Retail Theft,'" *The Guardian*, November
15, 2021, https://www.theguardian.com/
us-news/2021/nov/15/walgreens-closures-san-
francisco-crime-debate.

6. James Lindsay, "Groomer Schools 1: The Long
Cultural Marxist History of Sex Education,"
November 19, 2021, in *New Discourses*, podcast,
https://newdiscourses.com/2021/11/groomer-
schools-1-long-cultural-marxist-history-sex-
education/.

7. Lindsay, "Groomer Schools 1."

8. Yissilmissil Productions, "Fairfax High School
FCPS Board Meeting—Stacy Langton—
Citizen Participation 9-23-2021," YouTube,
October 10, 2021, https://www.youtube.com/
watch?v=ktF72zIyHp0.

9. Lindsay, "Groomer Schools 1."

10. "Stop Comprehensive Sex Education (CSE)," Child Protection League, accessed April 22, 2022, https://cplaction.com/CSE/.

11. "Sample of *It's Perfectly Normal* Curriculum," Child Protection League, accessed April 22, 2022, https://cplaction.com/health-sexuality/#pn.

12. Karl Marx and Frederick Engels, *Manifesto of the Communist Party* (London: Communist League, 1848), https://www.marxists.org/archive/marx/works/download/pdf/Manifesto.pdf.

13. "Advance Monthly Sales for Retail and Food Services," US Census Bureau, November 16, 2021, https://www.census.gov/retail/marts/www/marts_current.pdf.

14. "GDP Ranked by Country 2021," World Population Review, accessed April 22, 2022, https://worldpopulationreview.com/countries/countries-by-gdp.

<h2 style="text-align:center">Chapter 6</h2>

1. Emma Goldberg, "The New Chief Chaplain at Harvard? An Atheist," *New York Times*, August 26, 2021, https://www.nytimes.com/2021/08/26/us/harvard-chaplain-greg-epstein.html.

2. Leonardo Blair, "Study: Nearly 70% of Born-Again Christians Say Other Religions Can Lead to Heaven," *Aquila Report*, October 26, 2021, https://theaquilareport.com/study-nearly-70-of-born-again-christians-say-other-religions-can-lead-to-heaven/.

3. Beinzee, "A Gift of a Bible," YouTube.com, July 8, 2010, https://www.youtube.com/ watch?v=6md638smQd8, transcribed by the author.

Chapter 7

1. James Montgomery Boice, *Foundations of the Christian Faith, Revised and Expanded* (Downers Grove, IL: IVP Academic, 2019), 467.

Chapter 8

1. Francis X. Rocca, "Churches Push Back Against Coronavirus Restrictions," *Wall Street Journal*, November 20, 2020, https://www.wsj. com/articles/churches-push-back-against-coronavirus-restrictions-11605867870.
2. Elle Reynolds, "L.A. Threatens John MacArthur and His Church with Fines, Arrest for Holding Services," *The Federalist*, August 5, 2020, https:// thefederalist.com/2020/08/05/l-a-threatens-john-macarthur-and-his-church-with-fines-arrest-for-holding-services/.
3. Rocca, "Churches Push Back Against Coronavirus Restrictions."
4. Jeremy Weber, "Christian, What Do You Believe? Probably a Heresy About Jesus, Says Survey," *Christianity Today*, October 16, 2018, https://www.christianitytoday.com/news/2018/ october/what-do-christians-believe-ligonier-state-theology-heresy.html.

5. Elena Garcia, "Oprah's 'Church' Video Draws Over 5 Million to YouTube," *Christian Post*, April 23, 2008, https://www.christianpost.com/article/20080423/oprah-s-church-video-draws-over-5-million-to-youtube.htm.

6. Garcia, "Oprah's 'Church' Video Draws Over 5 Million to YouTube."

Connect with
Dr. Michael Youssef!

Follow Dr. Youssef for life-giving truth, behind-the-scenes ministry updates, and much more.

MichaelYoussef.com

 MichaelAYoussef

 Michael A. Youssef

Biblical Encouragement
for You—Anytime, Anywhere

Leading The Way with Dr. Michael Youssef is passionately proclaiming uncompromising Truth through every major form of media, empowering you to know and follow Christ. There are many FREE ways you can connect with Dr. Youssef's teachings:

- Thousands of sermons and articles online
- TV and radio programs worldwide
- Apps for your phone or tablet
- A monthly magazine, and more!

Learn more at **LTW.org/Connect**